MOM MADE US WRITE THIS IN THE SUMMER

Journal One
MAX and Maggie

MOM MADE US WRITE THIS IN THE SUMMER

Maggie

MAX

by ALI MAIER

Erie Island
MEDIA

Mom Made Us Write This in the Summer
Published by
Erie Island Media, LLC
2947 Interstate Parkway
Brunswick, OH 44212
www.erieislandmedia.com
www.mommadeuswritethis.com

Illustrations and interior design by Joanna Robinson, *jart1473.wix.com/joannarobinson*
Cover design by Monica Thomas for TLC Graphics, *www.TLCGraphics.com*

Publisher's Cataloging-in-Publication data

Maier, Ali.
   Mom made us write this in the summer / Ali Maier.
   p. cm.
   ISBN 9780989375504
   Series : Max and Maggie , Journal one.
   Summary : Twin siblings Max and Maggie Pruitt can't believe when mom makes them share a summer journal. A family oriented, he said - she said journal.
   [1. Twins—Fiction. 2. Family life—Fiction. 3. Siblings Fiction. 4. Diary fiction. 5. Summer—Fiction. 6. Ohio—Fiction.] I. Title. II. Series.

PZ7.M27756 Mom 2013
[Fic] — dc23   2013939362

First Printing: September 2013
Erie Island Media, LLC
Printed in the United States of America

For my family.
Thank you for the years
of love and laughter.

Dear Maggie and Max,

I bought this summer journal for you to share. I would like you to write about your summer. It will give you a wonderful opportunity to see things from each other's perspective.

Here are the rules:
1. You both must write at least 12 times over the summer.
2. You both must write about each topic.
3. Take turns choosing a topic. Whoever chooses the topic writes first.
4. You must read the previous entry before you begin to write.
5. You may write comments on each other's journal entries, but you must be polite.
6. Exceptional vocabulary will earn you extra allowance. (The words must be used correctly.)
7. Use this time to express yourself without interruption. Be honest and be yourself. You may disagree, but you may not be mean or rude to each other.

You are both very funny and talented writers, so I can't wait to read what you've written. I love you both!

Love, Mom

Brainstorming/Doodling Pages

Write about your feelings and thoughts!

Other ideas to write about:
Summertime: What are your favorite activities?
What do you like about them?

What are your brother's/sister's best qualities?
What are your best qualities?

What is something you need to work on as a sibling?

What do you hope to accomplish this summer?

What are you looking forward to about fifth grade?
What are you afraid of, if anything?
What do you hope to learn?

School: What are your favorite subjects and why?

What are your favorite family memories and why?

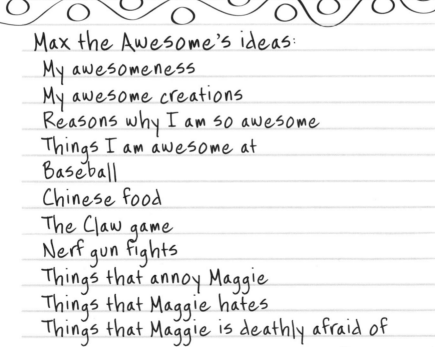

Maggie's ideas:
Things I love
Things I hate
Max's quirky habits
Zoo animals (:
ICE CREAM!
The mall!
Drawing cool things
Roller skating
What makes Max weird sometimes
Why Max is annoying sometimes

Max the Awesome's ideas:
My awesomeness
My awesome creations
Reasons why I am so awesome
Things I am awesome at
Baseball
Chinese food
The Claw game
Nerf gun fights
Things that annoy Maggie
Things that Maggie hates
Things that Maggie is deathly afraid of

Maggie's Guide to Writing a Journal that Mom will Like:

1. Think of cool ideas.   All my ideas are cool!

2. Draw awesome pictures.   That's your thing, not mine.

3. Make sure you write in full sentences and use good grammar, especially if Mom is going to read it.   Ugh.

4. If you don't know how to spell a word, look it up because Mom hates misspelled words.   Or just pick another word. That's what I do!

5. Add lots of doodles and scribbles, because they are cool.

    Doodles and scribbles?
    I can do that!

I think we need to do a countdown until we reach the last journal entry. Mom says we have to do 12. so this first one will be entry #12!

Good idea! I can't wait until we get to #1! Ugh! It seems so far away right now.

The Journal by Maggie

Grrrrr..... You ALWAYS use that excuse!

I will go first. Ladies first, right? Today is exactly the fifth day of summer vacation. Max and I are officially home for the summer. Ahhhhhhhh..... I just love summer!

Every day. Together. All day. A recipe for disaster, right? Actually, Max and I made it five whole days without arguing. Yep. Five whole days. It was wonderful. Really good. Unfortunately, it didn't last. Which is why I have to write this.

Max and Maggie tornado!!

Today, we were being lazy, lying on the couch, watching some morning TV. Mom called for us to come into the kitchen for a "talk." That is never a good sign.

No it is not...

Max and I looked at each other and cringed. We just knew something was up. "Having a talk" only happens when we are in trouble. Sometimes, Mom and Dad pretend that's not what "having a talk" is, but we know the truth.

Yep, we're onto them!

Mom may actually grade this when we are done...

We left our comfy spots on the couch, and went into the kitchen. I don't know about Max, but I was feeling pretty nervous. *ME TOO!!*

Mom was sitting at the kitchen table with a brand-new notebook. She had "a project" for us. That's the fun way of saying we would be doing some sort of school-type work. *Duhn, Duhn, DUHN!!*
(That's the sound they make in movies when something bad is about to happen.)

I guess I should have expected this for two reasons:

1. My mom used to teach English. She loves reading and writing, and anything to do with school. A lot. Plus, she thinks we should practice over the summer to stay on top of our work.

And the second reason...

2. Max and I get on each other's nerves.
Mom gets mad at us when we fight.
She is always looking for some way
to encourage us to get along. Max
was super-annoying ~~awesome~~ yesterday so she came
up with a brilliant idea to make us work
today.

or, you get on my nerves, mostly

awesome

That's the most ridiculous idea I have ever heard of!

At first, I was excited to see the
notebook. I thought I was getting some
new stuff. NEW STUFF—YAY! I love
presents!

Sometimes when Mom is out
shopping, she'll see a good deal on colored
pencils, stickers, markers, notepads, and
stuff like that. She will just buy it for
us, for no reason at all. She likes to give
us projects to do. I love that! I love to
doodle and draw and write. At least, I like
to write about fun stuff.

By fun you mean drawing a million pictures of animals and doodling everywhere...

I do like that stuff! You just always take it before I have a chance.

So, I love a brand-new, clean notebook. And I thought for sure it must be for me, because Max doesn't like that stuff as much. He always gets stuff like rubber bands, paper clips, and other non-writing stuff. But paper? Because you can make cool stuff with all of that awesomeness. Duh!

Totally for me, right?
WRONG!

We spent the next half hour listening to my mom talk about how Max and I have trouble communicating. My mom decided that we should take turns writing in a journal all summer so we understand each other better.

We communicate like we are 4!

HEY! I'm not sure anything can make me understand Max better, but whatever. It's not like I have a choice here. ← No kidding.

Really? You like expressing your opinion? I hadn't noticed. Ha ha - NOT!

I do love expressing my opinion, so I guess that part could be fun. Anyway, it's supposed to make us fight less somehow. I am seriously not sure I get how that is supposed to work, but I will give it a shot.

Max and I are twins. We just finished 4th grade. We live together. We go to school together. We have the same friends. blah. blah. blah. We are practically connected at the hip — not by choice though.

Just so you know, it's not my choice either!

It is almost impossible NOT to argue when we spend so much time together. We're bound to drive each other crazy at times.

I may have to frame this.

Awwww. I knew you liked me.

It's not that we don't like each other. Really. I may be one of the few sisters in the world who actually likes her brother. I don't know if it's because we're twins or what, but we are pretty close friends. He still gets annoying sometimes. Actually, he's pretty funny when he's not being annoying.

Awesome

It's just that we're together all the time, and it's hard to spend that much time with someone and NOT get annoyed with them.

Because we are twins, people always talk about us interchangeably, even though we are nothing alike. Even my mom can't remember who I am half the time. She calls me Max almost as often as she calls me Maggie. Maybe if we were both girls, I would not be so offended by that, but really. In case you haven't noticed...

I KNOW!

Just so you know, I am offended by that, too.

Max is a BOY. I am a GIRL.

HELLOOOOOO!

UUUGH.

Anyway, about being twins...

But I am taller. And Awesomer!

I'm older, by a few minutes at least. The twin thing was kind of cute when we were little. Twins get extra attention for some reason. I don't know why, but I used to really like it. People would look at us when we were little, and tell us how adorable we were and give us things, just because we were born the same day. It never really made sense to me, because being twins really didn't take any special skill on our part, but the attention was nice.

That's not even a word, Max!

Maggie LOVES attention!

• Summer •

11

Now things are different. Being a twin has its drawbacks. The most annoying thing is that all of our teachers think we are the same. Hello!? We are not the same! I am creative. I like to draw and write. I'm great at writing stories, but I do not like math. At all. It's some kind of torture, invented just to make my life a living nightmare.

It's more like you don't put ANY time into it!

I think that I am pretty smart, except for math. I do OK in school. I just don't like to put a lot of time into it. Sometimes I forget things, so my grades are typically B's with a few A's thrown in. OK, and maybe, just maybe a C once in a while on my report card. (Although that did not end well for me. That's another story *I remember that day. SO glad it wasn't me!* altogether.)

Look out! The zombie numbers are chasing you, Maggie! They are out to get you!

VERY funny, Max.

This is
totally
TRUE.

Well, Max is, like, super smart. He
actually studies. He is in advanced in like...
EVERYTHING. He's the guy who scores in
the 99th percentile on those long tests
they make you take once or twice a year
at school. You know, the ones that totally
make your teachers freak out? Anyway,
Max is crazy smart, and that's just
ridiculous.

This is
totally
TRUE,
too.

That puts me in a tough spot. If I went
to school all by myself, like a normal,
non-twin person, I would be cruising along,
doing average to pretty well in school, and
no one would really notice me. I would be a
good-enough student. Instead, I am constantly
judged and compared to Mr. Perfect. All of
our teachers just LOVE Max, and I find
it very annoying.

This is
totally
TRUE
too

That's me!

At least I am the CUTE one in the
family.

I can't help
it. Teachers
DO love me.
And, really,
what's not
to love?

yeah right!

So that was my first shot at journal writing. Oh yeah, I think I was supposed to write how I feel about writing this journal, so I had better do that.

I am unhappy about having to do school-ish work in the summer.

I am confused about how this is supposed to make a difference in how Max and I get along.

ME TOO!

Plus, I am a little nervous that Max is going to be a jerk when he reads what I wrote.

But I am happy that I get to pick what we write about half the time.

HEY! Me? A jerk? Never!

(By the way, I'm thinking of things already. I may make Max write about going to the mall or something that he hates, just to see what he does ! Ha Ha!)

Nice. I can't wait to get these awesome topics to write about.

The Journal by MAX (the Awesome)

← Really?

Let me first start by saying UGH. This stinks. Like elephants. Or penguins. While every other kid is relaxing all summer, I am doing schoolwork. I know, party time, right?!?

Apparently, my sister and I do not "communicate well." That is a quote from my mom, who also said she will not spend her summer "listening to the two of us argue constantly." What's her brilliant solution? Writing homework. Great. Most kids are celebrating the end of schoolwork, and I am spending my time writing in this journal.

Doesn't seem fair, does it? NOPE!

Summer homework=brain poison

HA! Good one, Max!

Ummm... you mean A LOT!

My mom used to be a teacher, so she's a (little) obsessed with reading and writing. Figures. Even when we were very small, we would read all the time. Most people listen to music in the car. We listen to books on CD. We even have tons of books on our iPods, and we own about a million books. Our house is a library. We probably have more books than the library at school. It's <u>crazy.</u> actually... it's awesome.

Our house: Normal house:

I can't say I'm surprised about this, but it doesn't mean I have to like the idea. This project is right up Mom's alley. Maggie's, too. She pretends she doesn't like this idea, but she really does.

HEY! I don't want to write this either!

Apparently, Mom thinks a journal will help me learn to get along with Maggie and improve my writing skills at the same time. Whatever. I think I heard the word "vocabulary" in there, too. Ugh.

Is that even possible ???

It is summer. I plan to sleep in, play video games, and hang out with some friends sometimes. That works for me. What I do NOT plan to do is let my sister tell me what to do every second of every day. And I do not plan to get in trouble, while Maggie stands there acting all innocent. I don't ACT innocent. I AM innocent.

I only tell you what to do when you are being annoying.

Correction: YOU got us in trouble yesterday!

We got in trouble yesterday, and I'm pretty sure that's when my mom got the idea for this journal. I could see it in her eyes. That is why I am sitting in my room writing this instead of doing what I want to do.

MAX is GREAT → *ridiculous*

Here's what happened: We were just watching some show on TV, and we were both kinda bored. I found my favorite nerf gun and a few stray bullets as I was walking to the kitchen for a snack, and I got an idea. I snuck upstairs and loaded up. I threw on some camo clothes, just for effect. I put on my goggles and slithered back down the stairs. Not easy with that creaky fifth step. It takes stealth-like skills to pull off the plan I had in mind.

Really? You needed to get camo to shoot me?

There is a clear view of where Maggie was sitting from the bottom of the stairs:

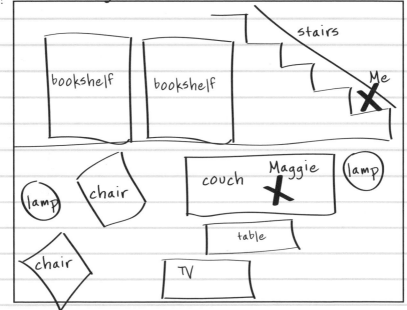

Are you kidding?

I moved like the most talented ninja, so she didn't see me. I snuck around with my back to the wall, then hit the ground. I belly-crawled into the family room and around the back of the couch until I could get a clear view of her. Maggie was just sitting there, watching TV, eating a bowl of cereal. Unsuspecting!

Yeah. By the way, thanks for ruining my food. I couldn't finish my breakfast with your disgusting bullets floating in the milk.

Totally innocent!

Then I shot her. Not one, but two, three, four, five, six times.
I totally pummeled her!!! One bullet even bounced off her face and landed in her cereal. Hysterical!!! I practically wet my pants because I was laughing so hard.
I wish you would have wet your pants. Now THAT would have been funny... no wait —hysterical!

LOL!

To recap, all I did was shoot Maggie a couple of times with my nerf gun. She was just lying there, and the bullets are foam, so they don't even hurt. It was funny.

I don't know why she got all mad. It could have been a lot worse because I have a gigantic arsenal of things that I can shoot. I have rubber band guns, foam bow-and-arrow sets, and every kind of nerf shooter they make.

I even have a rubber band cannon that I got at the fair last summer. It is seriously **cool.**

MAX

The next thing I knew, Maggie was screaming at me and Mom came running in, angry that we interrupted her while she was working. I'm pretty sure that was the exact moment that Mom decided something must be done about us, and this journal thing was born.

SEE!!! Totally your fault!

The shots don't even hurt. They are foam, and we shoot each other all the time, but today, Maggie started yelling at me.

Those bullets DO hurt!

All I was trying to do was to liven up our day a little, but Maggie totally freaked out. Then Mom totally freaked out.

I did not freak out!

Maggie freaking out

MOM freaking out

And now, I have schoolwork to do all summer long. Great.

I wish Dad stayed home during the day. He loves to have nerf wars with me. And whenever Maggie gets mad, he teases her until she laughs. He makes the days much more fun. Plus, he's great at distracting Mom when she gets annoyed with us, so we don't get in trouble. I guess he can make Mom laugh when she's mad, too.

Yeah. and that's so NOT funny!

Good luck with that...

That really is a talent. I need to learn that trick, too. I should ask him about that when he gets home from work tonight... I wonder if he knows about this journal thing. Probably not. Oh, he knows. He just won't argue with her when she decides something.

Only

journal entries
left to write!

summer

The Zoo by the Amazing Max

My turn to pick what we write about.
Oh yeah. I had planned on writing about my
baseball practice last night, but this morning
we went to the zoo, and I saw something
hysterical, and it changed my mind.

I can't believe you don't like animals. You're nuts.

Here goes...

OK, so I don't usually like the zoo, right?
Let me start by saying that zoos are usually
pretty disgusting. They smell gross, and most
of the animals just lie there and ignore you. It
is not really that entertaining. I have to admit
I had pretty low expectations of how our zoo
trip was going to go.

The day started like any other zoo day.
Lots of animals, lots of weird stinky smells, etc.
But of course, I have no choice. I get dragged
along. To see the same things, every time.
Over and over and over and over again.
And over and over and over...
you get the idea.

And you complain over and over and over again!

Maggie and my mom LOVE the zoo, like, over-the-top kind of love. Maggie takes a thousand pictures, and Mom says, "Awwww... isn't it cute," about a million times. I just walk along, trying not to get in trouble.

Because it is totally cool!

Clearly, I'm not as crazy about animals as they are.

Plus, it smells. Bad. Really bad. Especially the penguins. Who knew a bird could make that kind of stink?

OK Penguins do stink. but they are so funny!

So, the whole day was starting out just as I expected. One boring animal after another, like any other zoo trip. We spent forever looking at animal after animal after animal. My sister took thousands of pictures. We walked and walked. Mom oooed and awwwed.

Aw! Sea lions! I love sea lions!

SO, right next to the sea lions and seals they have a guy with a little cart that looks like it should be full of ice cream or something delicious. (I love getting snacks from those stands at the zoo, the amusement park, or the mall.) Anyway, it looked like a snack stand, so I started to think "Hey, I could have a snack, maybe this day is looking better..." Then we got closer, and you realize that the snack stand is really full of DEAD FISH. That's right. Dead FISH. I may write it again, just to make sure my severe disappointment is understood.

You drew dead fish? really? ew.

DEAD FISH.

Why are you always thinking about food?

Anyway, instead of getting a cool, delicious ice cream or some other fantastic snack/junk food, I was given a cup of dead fish. So, I threw dead fish at the sea lions. I mean TO the sea lions. (wink, wink, nod, nod...) So then my hands smelled like disgusting fish, and the stink wouldn't wash away. It was pretty gross. Yet another disappointment at the zoo.

I knew you were trying to hit them with the fish! You are so mean!

After all of that, I thought for sure it was going to be yet another blah day. But then something happened that was so funny, it may have made up for all the boring, stinky trips we've had to the zoo. My stomach still hurts from laughing. Seriously, today I saw the funniest thing I've ever seen in my life.

I was walking along, pretending to be interested in the boring facts Mom kept reading on the signs, and it happened right in front of us.

I may have to take a break from writing, because I can't stop laughing. We were standing there, looking at the hippos. There were three of them. One was a baby, so the other two must have been the mom and dad. I'm not sure. The baby and mom were doing something. I don't know what, because I wasn't looking at them. Probably eating, because really, what else do animals do besides stand around and eat?

I was looking right at the big daddy hippo. He was HUGE. He was standing near the pond with his butt facing me. There were a few birds walking around, and I thought, if I were a bird, I don't think I'd stand out next to some humongously huge animal that could crush me in a second. Birds are not very smart. But that's not the funny part.

Hippos and birds are friends!

I think I need a drumroll for the funny part. [Imagine a drumroll here.]

Drumroll! Ha! Good one, Max!

All of a sudden, the hippo's tail started twitching back and forth. I heard this noise, but I couldn't tell where it was coming from. Then the tail twitched more, and I realized the hippo was farting. He was farting and farting and farting so loud that it echoed through the zoo!! His tail flew back and forth. Then there were little pieces of hippo poop flying left and right with every wiggle of his tail!

I cannot believe I have to read this.

The fart sounds continued for, like, 5 minutes, the tail wagged back and forth, and the poop flew everywhere! I've never seen anything like it. It was disgustingly hysterical!

This is so gross! I can't believe you actually wrote about it and drew pictures. Ick. No, double ick.

Max, you are so disgusting!

EW!

hippo poop

HIPPO FARTS

are the funniest thing ever.
(And the best thing about the zoo.)

more hippo poop

I have never laughed so hard in my life. Who knew hippos could fart like that? They may be my new favorite animal. Maybe the zoo isn't so bad. Animals are gross, but animal farts are definitely funny.

We have a cousin who has a great zoo story. She's my grandpa's cousin or something like that, so we're related somehow. She got hit with lion pee at a zoo when she was little. I can't remember exactly what happened, but watching her tell the whole story is hysterical. That was the best thing I had ever heard about happening at the zoo before today.
I can't wait to tell her about hippo farts.

That is disgusting!
I'm going to have
nightmares about
that. Thanks a lot.

Max's Guide to the Zoo:

1. Stay away from the penguin house.
They stink. Really bad. Max, you don't always
smell like roses.

2. Do not buy the fish to feed the sea
lions. The stink from this fish will stay on
your hands and will not wash off for days.
Ha! Serves you right for
throwing fish AT them!

3. Always investigate if you hear a weird
noise. You never know if something
hysterical is happening. (I just learned
this rule today!)

I just have one thing to add to this guide:

4. If you can avoid it, do not take Max
to the zoo with you. Leave him at
home. Trust me, you will be
much happier!

THE ZOO

by Maggie

You mean, hysterical!

Of all of the cool things we saw at the zoo today, I cannot believe that my brother wrote about the hippo farting. That was so gross. I don't know how he possibly could have thought it was funny. Max is grossed out by everything, except what is actually gross. I will never make sense of that!

Sometimes there's a fine line between disgusting and funny.

Max tolerates the zoo because he has to, but sometimes he complains and complains until Mom yells at him and gets mad. Today he didn't complain too much. I'm glad, because he can really ruin a trip to the zoo if he grumps around all day. Then Mom gets mad, and ugh. It's just not good.

Because I am bored out of my mind!

This is Max when he saw hippo farts.

Mom and I love the zoo. Our zoo is really awesome. There is a rainforest that is all inside, so we go there a lot in the winter when it's too cold to be outside. If you go there when it's snowing outside, it feels like you're in a reverse snow globe, warm and cozy inside, looking out of a big glass dome at the snow falling outside. It is really cool. That is one of my favorite times at the zoo.

I like to take pictures of the animals, especially if they are doing something weird or funny. Maybe I'll be some type of animal photographer when I'm older. My parents let me use their good camera so I get some great shots. I have about a thousand pictures on my computer at home.

It's more like a gazillion pictures.

i ♡ meerkats!

The meerkats are so funny. I love how they run around, stand up on their back legs, with their tiny little arms held up, and look around. Then they run somewhere else and do the same thing. They are hilarious. I could watch them for hours!

Agreed.
Meerkats are funny.
And they don't even smell bad!

I don't understand why some animals do weird things or have such weird parts. Like, how could a T-Rex have actually had such mini arms?

Some weird parts make sense, like a giraffe's long neck. They have a crazy long neck to reach into the trees to eat.

But why would penguins have such mini legs? Crazy. That's what makes animals so cool — all those weird things.

I think it would be fun to write a whole book about weird animal parts.

I can't believe you actually spend time thinking about this stuff. You are strange, Maggie.

Ok, this whole page is just plain weird.

Don't say that! It will turn into more homework! AAAHHH!

Today Mom bought us little cups of nectar to feed the birds. They were lorikeets, and they were very cool. Their feathers were bright blue, green, yellow, and orange. When you hold out the cup of nectar, they fly over and eat right out of the cup while you are holding it! I am not usually a big fan of birds, but feeding them was kinda cool.

I actually had 3 lorikeets feeding from my cup until this annoying kid showed up. He was running around like a Tasmanian devil, screaming and chasing all the birds away. It was so annoying. I guess his parents thought he was being cute.

I've got news for you — he's NOT cute.

That kid was super annoying! He was like a wild animal!

My favorite animals are the big cats. They are so pretty and I love to draw them. Last summer, we had two baby tiger cubs at our zoo. They were so cute. It was funny watching them roll around and play together.

I was thinking that they were lucky that there were two of them. When the mom tiger wanted to be left alone, the cubs had each other to play with.

Baby tigers playing = SO adorable. Cutest. Thing. Ever. It made me think of Max and me, except not as cute! As much as we bug each other, it is always nice to have each other.

This is true. It is good to have each other. You are very lucky to have me. AND, without you, who would I use for target practice?

Big cats are so cool!

I love them!

I wish we had a cat.
Or two.
Or three.

NO WAY!
No animals
allowed in
our house!

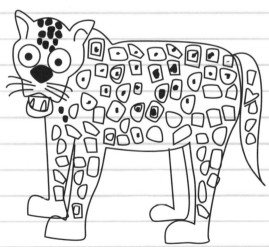

We watched the penguins for a while, too. It's one of the few birds I actually like. They are so funny to watch. They waddle around. They slip around on their stomachs instead of walking. I think if I were a penguin, I would slide around on my stomach all the time. I think it would be frustrating to waddle on those tiny little short legs. I would probably try to go too fast and trip. Graceful, I am not. Belly sliding — yep. That would totally be the way to go.

Penguins: A.K.A
(also known as) THE
smelliest animals
EVER!

True.
You are
clumsy.
I agree
with that
100%.

Penguins can also go from swimming in the water, to standing in the snow, like, in a second. They just fly out of the water like a torpedo and land right on their feet. That is totally cool.

Of course, Max acted like he was going to die while we were in the penguin house. It really does stink in there, but suck it up. Max acted like the smell might actually kill him. And yet, he thinks any type of fart is hysterical. It is very hard to understand a brother.

No lie -
It REALLY SMELLED.
I really did almost die from the stink in there.
I seriously could not breathe.

Note to self: bring gas mask to the zoo next time.

We only have...

more to go!

Aaaaaaaaarrrggg!!!

I am so annoyed. and furious and mad.
MAYBE I SHOULD WRITE IN ALL CAPS TO
SHOW HOW IRRITATED I AM.

Alright. When people say writing
in all caps means you're yelling, it is
clearly not true. I just tried it. and
it doesn't feel like I am yelling at all!
No satisfaction from capital letters.

Aaaaaaaaarrrggg!!!

I also do not know how to yell when I
write without sounding like a ridiculous
pirate. Infuriating.

OK. I will take a deep breath and try
to explain what just happened. It was a
typical morning. We had nothing to do
today. I had this great plan of doing
nothing — lying around. watching TV.
texting my friends — the perfect.
do-nothing kind of day.

Today also happens to be a workday for my mom. She only works part-time, although don't use the word "only" if you are talking to her. Somehow, that is offensive, although I don't really know why. She goes into an office for meetings sometimes, but usually she works at home. Her desk has about a million papers and books on it. She says she gets lost in her work. I can see why.

no kidding!

Unfortunately for Max and me, that "office" is also in the living room, which is not far from the family room, which is where we like to hang out. We also have a basement where we can go, but I don't like being down there during the day. It makes me feel like I'm in a cave. Max likes the basement during the day, but not at night. He's even too afraid to go down there.

The basement is cool - that's where all the video games are!

It IS a cave - a man cave. Girls wouldn't like it!

I'm not afraid!

Summer

When Mom is working at home, cooperating and giving her space can be a challenge, to say the least. We try to be quiet and let her work, but it doesn't always happen.

Today's problem started when I was watching TV. I woke up first, as usual, so I had the remote. I was lying on the couch when Max woke up and came downstairs. He lay down on the small couch, like always.

So, if you know this, why don't you leave me alone?

This is because I AM still asleep!

For the first half hour or so after waking up, Max is in a zombie-like state. He just lies there and stares into space. I'm not even sure he can talk during this period. I've never heard or seen it happen. My mom and dad used to try to talk to him in the morning, but finally, after years and years of blank stares, they figured out it's best to leave him alone.

Zombie MAX

Very funny. I do not have polka-dot pajamas.

Don't you mean, opinions are fine as long as they're yours?

So everything was fine until Max slipped out of his morning-coma and had to have an opinion on what we were watching. ☆Opinions are fine, as long as they are not dumb. Anyway, he started to make me crazy. Anyone who has had a sibling can understand. We began to argue a bit. Well, we must have gotten a little loud and Mom was on a work call and they could hear us arguing! When Mom got off the phone, we were in trouble.

Mom told us it was embarrassing to be talking to a customer with us behaving like that. She also said she would not be able to work at home if we continued to be loud and obnoxious. I don't want my mom to have a hard time working from home.

I wouldn't get to sleep in!?!?! That would be awful.

I think we're lucky to get to stay home during the summer. I have friends whose moms have to go to work every day. They have to get up early and go to daycare or their grandma's, or their neighbor's house. Even in the summer. They don't get to stay home during the day.

Sometimes it seems fun, because you would never get bored if you were around a bunch of other kids every day, but I think I like that I can wake up whenever I want and be home during the day. I like being able to sleep in, and to lie around in my pajamas as long as I want.

I agree. Sweet summer freedom!

Anyway, I don't want Mom to lose her job, and I really don't want to be the reason she can't work from home anymore. I felt bad for interrupting her while she worked, and she felt bad for getting so upset, and I'm pretty sure that Max felt nothing. Not true. I felt confused. Still do.

We spent a long, long time talking about what we did wrong, and how important it is to be quiet while Mom is working and so on. I felt terrible and sorry, and I cried a little. Then Mom cried too, and we hugged. This whole situation did NOT require tears... I'm pretty sure. Dad would have thought all the crying was ridiculous, too...

You're mad at me? Huh? What for?

My lovely brother Max just stood there without a care, looking at my mom and me like we were crazy. It made me furious. So now, I am totally mad at him. I am also annoyed, angry, and frustrated, and I want to scream at him, but I don't want to bother Mom again.

Not true. I did care, you two just overreacted...

So, I am writing angrily.

Hee hee (just kidding!)

IN CAPITAL MAD

LETTERS TO GET OUT

MY FRUSTRATION!!!!

Mad Maggie

veins popping out of her neck

smoke coming from her ears

OK, OK, I'm sorry!

(Although I'm not really sure what I am apologizing for.)

(I have to say that I do feel a little better after writing all that. However, it doesn't change the fact that I am still mad at Max, and I probably will be for a while.)

Girls and grudges. Geez, oh man!

Maggie's Guide to NOT Getting in Trouble:

1. Ask people for things. Don't just grab stuff.

2. Do not shoot people with stuff.

3. Don't complain all the time.

If Max could follow these simple rules, we would pretty much never get in trouble.

Yeah, right.

Max's Guide to Dealing with Mom and Dad-

Every kid gets in trouble sometimes. Here are the rules to follow to make trouble less painful for the kid (victim).

1. Sit down. The more parents have to look down at you when they are mad, the better. It's a way to remind them that you are still just a kid, and you are smaller than them. Find a seat immediately. Standing up makes you seem bigger, like you should know better than to have done whatever it is that you did.

2. Do not make eye contact. It's a sign of defiance. Have you ever watched those animal shows on TV? The ones that tell you how to escape wild animals? Maggie makes me watch that stuff. Well, the same rules apply here. Eye contact makes it look like you are challenging them. Parents hate that.

Are you saying that Mom and Dad are like wild animals?

See the next page for more tips...

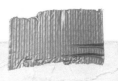

3. Hang your head pitifully, fold your hands in your lap (sometimes I use prayer-style hands to remind them how good I am) and whatever you do, DO NOT SMILE.

4. THE MOST IMPORTANT RULE - Never make eye contact with your sister during this time, because she can make you laugh. Laughing when you are getting yelled at is the absolute worst thing you can do.

Getting in Trouble

By Max (the ~~Incredible~~) Clueless

Ummmm... All I can say is:

How can you be so smart and so clueless at the same time?

TOTAL OVERREACTION.

I'm not even exactly sure what happened. One minute I'm watching TV. The next minute Mom is mad at us, and the next minute Mom and Maggie are crying and hugging each other. I was not trying to make Maggie mad, I just have no idea what just happened.

My point exactly! You are totally clueless!

?

I got up, and my sister and my mom were in kind of bad moods. My mom has a big project due next week, so she's been working a lot, and that makes her pretty stressed out. I get that. At least Mom has an excuse. I have no idea why Maggie was such a grump. It was just one of those days. I was wishing I had gone to work with my dad.

I was not a grump!

I wish you would have gone to work with Dad, too!

It started with the TV. Mags and I were watching TV. I got up and ~~grabbed the remote.~~ Maggie wasn't fast-forwarding through the commercials.

That is SO annoying.

dramatically ripped the remote from Maggie's sweet, innocent hands...

Why watch commercials if the show is recorded, and you don't have to? Maggie was distracted, and I grabbed the remote. That is all I did!

Usually, this is no big deal. Maggie is typically multitasking when she watches TV, anyway. She is always texting her friends, using the computer, reading... whatever. She's not paying enough attention to the TV to fast-forward past the stupid commercials.

It is usually no big deal because it is sitting on the table. When it is in my hands - NOT OK to grab!

So I was stuck watching some underwear commercial. Watching a bunch of guys hanging out in their underwear is truly disturbing. Seriously?! You can't blame me for wanting to fast-forward.

That is gross. See, Max. I do agree with you about something!

This is why I am:

MASTER OF THE REMOTE
also known as
KING OF THE REMOTE

(At least when my dad is not home). When Dad and I watch TV, we watch TV. The only distractions for us are snacks, and snacks don't prevent you from fast-forwarding when there is a commercial on.

because she was too busy being awesome! (:

➤

Maggie wasn't paying attention so I grabbed the remote. She acted like I had stabbed her with a pencil or something. All I did was grab the remote. Geez.

Maggie had that angry look in her eyes that reminds me of Mom when she's upset.
Then there was a scuffle.
Which turned into a brawl.
Which turned into a shouting match.
Which turned into us getting into big trouble.

You exaggerate, Max!

Little do you know that all you have to do is ASK for the remote. and I would gladly give it to you. Not that hard.

Unfortunately, the sounds of our little fight floated into the other room, where my mother was trying to work. That is never good. We really have to stay out of Mom's way when she's working.

Mom came in, and was upset. I guess she was on the phone, and we ruined her meeting. She talked to us a long time about her job, and the next thing I know, Maggie has tears in her eyes and my mom was crying too, and they were hugging each other. Then Mom pulled me into the hug and squeezed me while they cried. I really have no idea why anyone was crying. Maybe I missed something.

I'll say you missed something!

Seriously?!?!? You have no idea? How is that possible?

Then Mom kissed us both and went back to work in the other room.
I looked at Maggie, dumbfounded. She got mad and told me how mean I am. Then she stomped off.

The good news was, I got to watch TV by myself while Maggie did her journal. I thought maybe it would make more sense to me after I read Maggie's journal entry. That is the whole reason for all this writing, right? But I just read it, and I am still completely confused.

I guess some boys will never learn. Totally frustrating.

Personally, I think Maggie totally overreacted when I grabbed the remote. I still do not know why they were crying, and I have no idea why Maggie is so mad at me.

Aaaaargh!

You make me crazy sometimes! Like right now!!

This is Maggie when she is angry and sounds like a pirate! Her name is Swashbuckler Pruitt! HA!

3 journal entries done and only

more to go!

The Doctor By Max the Brave

Today is doctor day. Maggie is there now, so I am home writing. I kind of wish I was there at the same time because Maggie totally freaks out at the doctor's office. It is really funny. I don't know why, but as soon as she gets to the doctor's office, she turns into a crazy person. It's hilarious. Dr. J is really nice. He has this crazy long name I can't remember, but he lets us call him Dr. J.

OMG! I can't believe you are writing about what I think you are writing about. Thanks a lot. Max.

I don't mind going to see the doctor, because I like to hear how awesome I am, and Dr. J ALWAYS tells me. But Maggie hates the doctor's office. I bet she'll be mad when she sees what I wrote about today, but it is seriously SO FUNNY, I had to do it. She needs to learn not to take herself so seriously!

This is true. Max loves that.

Nice. You knew I'd be mad. and yet that did not stop you from writing about it.

I really really really really really really really dislike going to the doctor.
Really. That's not even enough reallys
to tell how much I do not like going to the doctor.

When we were little, Maggie threw a massive fit at the doctor's office. Every time we go there, they joke about how she's the only patient to ever put a hole in the wall of the examining room. Maggie gets totally embarrassed if we talk about it. Therefore, I am totally going to write about it.

NO

Well, aren't you a great brother?

Here's what happened:

When we were about 5 or 6, Mom took us to Dr. J's for a checkup. Mom never said the word "shot," but Maggie was pretty sure she was getting a shot if she went to the doctor, and Maggie is terrified of shots. Maggie was so scared but we were rushing around, so my mom really didn't even notice the panicked look on Maggie's face.

THis is the BEFORE picture. (before we even had our exams)

I hate the waiting room. Snotty-nosed babies and people coughing all over. Ick.

We waited in the waiting room, and Maggie was getting more and more scared. The nurse came out and called our names. We followed her into the back. She made us stand on a scale and checked how tall we were, the whole time commenting on how big we were getting.

Then she took us down a long hall, past a bunch of closed doors. There were other kids crying on the other side of the doors. We could hear them, and I'm sure that didn't help Maggie feel any better.

Kids were screaming at the top of their lungs! It was like a Halloween House of Horrors!

The nurse took us into one of the rooms. It had a hospitalish bed with a long piece of white paper covering it. There were two chairs for the parents to sit in, and a round, rolling chair for the doctor, and a long bed for the patient. I have always wanted a rolling chair like that.

Hate this too.

The rolling chair is. like. the ONLY thing I like about the doctor's office.

Anyway...

As soon as we got into the exam room, Maggie hid in the only place she could find, under the chairs. She squeezed herself into the smallest possible space, and just hid there. The nurse and my mom laughed so hard. She was like a scared puppy at the vet!

It was the only place to hide!

This is Maggie under the chair, still completely petrified.

Now I know what people mean when they say someone looks like they have seen a ghost. That's exactly how Maggie looked!

Thank you so much for making me relive this horrible experience in your play-by-play story with pictures! You are soooo thoughtful. (Can you tell I'm being sarcastic?) You probably can't tell because you are clueless!

I HATE shots. Yep. Hate 'em!

Mom said I should go first, so Maggie could see that a checkup is really easy and relatively painless. So, I jumped up onto the bed. I wasn't nervous at all. Shots don't feel good, but they are not that big of a deal.

I had my checkup, you know, all the basic stuff you do every time. The doctor feels your belly and your back, looks into your ears and down your throat. And up your nose — which is gross, but it didn't hurt.

Add that to my list of things I hate about the doctor's office:
I hate the nose exam.

Then he hits your knee with that weird little hammer and your leg kicks out all by itself — like you have no control! That feels really strange! I'm glad I didn't kick Dr. J.

Oh, yeah! I hate that little hammer thing too. Thanks for reminding me.

I could see Maggie peeking out from under the chair at me the whole time. I tried to make it look easy, which wasn't hard, because it WAS easy. I was really trying to be a good brother.

yeah, right!

When I finished my turn, it was time for Maggie to come out. It was pretty funny, because I'm not sure that Dr. J even noticed her under the chair until my mom started to tug on her. Mom started to drag Maggie out from under the chair, but she wouldn't budge.

The doctor tried to lift the chair off her, but Maggie wrapped herself around the chair's legs, so they couldn't pull it away from her. She was like an octopus wrapped around the legs of the chair, and she was not about to let go!

Maggie (a.k.a. The Octopus) at the doctors office

Thanks. Max. That's another beautiful picture of me.

Just remember how strong I am the next time you mess with me.

Max rocks...

This is Max.

There was a lot of chaos for a while. It was crazy. It was like Maggie had 8 arms. Every time they would get one arm or leg free, another one would wrap around the chair. In the end, it took 3 nurses, the doctor and my mom to separate Maggie from her hiding spot.

Notice the ginormous head. You sure do love yourself, Max!

All of the adults looked exhausted and sweaty afterward, with their clothes all rumpled up and their hair messy and sticking to their faces. Dr. J had to crawl around on the floor afterward to find his heart-listening thing that usually hangs around his neck.

Duh. It's called a stethoscope! Even I know that.

Let's just say...Max.
That appointment did not go well.
As it turned out, we didn't even have to get shots that day. Maggie freaked out for nothing.

I still hate everything about the doctor's office, even if we don't have to get shots.

We still have the same doctor, and that doctor still has the same nurses working in the office. Maggie really must have left a lasting impression on all of them, because they bring it up every time we go there. Maggie never liked going to the doctor, but now it is extra embarrassing for her because they always bring up "the incident." And thank you for embarrassing me even more. What a great brother you are.

I think she should just let it go and laugh about it like the rest of us, but she gets all mad every time we go there. Plus, I think she is still afraid of shots! Yes. I am still afraid of shots! And maybe you should all just stop bringing it up! I mean. why don't adults notice when you don't want to talk about something? Brothers too — it's like they want you to be embarrassed all over again. NOT cool.

 **Max still rocks...** Get over yourself. Max!

Max's Guide to Visiting the Doctor –

1. Do what the doctor and your mom or dad say.

2. Get it over with.

3. Feel better.   Easier said than done. Max!

4. The end.

Maggie's Guide to Visiting the Doctor (equally as simple as Max's guide. but much safer!)

1. Run away.

2. Hide.

3. Protect your skin.

4. Cover your ears. nose. eyes and mouth. They are not safe.

EVIL. Torturous. Pain-Inducing
The Dreaded ∧ Doctor   By Maggie

Leave it to my brother to make me write about something I really can't stand. I hate going to the doctor's office. I hate, hate, hate, hate it. I have never liked it. I really dislike going to the doctor. REALLY. So thank you very much for making me write about it. Max.   You're so welcome! I knew you'd love it!

Here's why I hate the doctor's office:
1. I hate the stupid "gown" they give you — it is a giant paper towel, not clothes.
2. I do not like the way the doctor talks to your mom, like you're not even there.
3. I do not like blood.
4. I do not like to be poked and squeezed.
5. I hate the smell of the doctor's office. bleck. Look who's freaking out about smells now! Ha!
6. I hate the medical tools hanging on the wall.
7. I hate the trash can that is just for needles.
8. I hate that little hammer thing.
9. I absolutely, positively HATE shots.
10. I hate the waiting room. One word: disgusting.

Shall I go on?

Summer

I can't take it. I really hate shots. I mean, I really, really, really hate shots. Who actually likes shots? They're dreadful.

zis won't hurt a bit. Hold ztill my zweet little patient...

This is not what Dr. J looks like at all!

BWAH HA HA HA!!!!

[Imagine that really evil doctor laugh here]

Seriously? Maggie — it's not that bad!

Lucky for me (NOT), my mom is all over the annual checkup thing. She never misses a year. I think the idea that kids need a checkup every year is a little excessive.

Maybe babies should go, because their heads are still soft and they have serious drooling problems. But why do I still have to go? I am perfectly healthy. I hardly ever get sick. Why should I have to go every year? It just doesn't make sense.

My dad told me that my grandma used to forge doctors' signatures ← *Isn't that illegal?* when he was a kid. You know the form that a doctor is supposed to fill in before you can play a sport? She'd say, "You're fine, you don't need to go to the doctor," and she would sign the forms herself with a messy signature, and that would be that.

No embarrassing moments sitting in a cold room wrapped in a thing they call a gown but is really just a long, shirt-shaped paper towel. My mom is so mad that Dad ever told us that. According to my dad, Mom is a "rule-follower," and if someone, somewhere says kids should have a checkup every year, you can be sure that is exactly what Mom will make us do.

Mom was so mad when she found out Dad told us that!

The only good news is that this year, Max and I had separate appointments. For years, we would go in together and take turns getting weighed and checked. Max always made me look bad, because he has no fear of sitting in a room half-naked, wearing a napkin and having someone jab a long, sharp needle into his skin.

I did not try to make you look bad on purpose. My awesomeness just sort of seeps out. I can't control it.

We had a huge health unit at school last year on your body. I learned that your skin is your largest organ. The whole purpose of having skin is to protect everything inside your body from all the stuff that is outside your body. I fail to see how shooting some mysterious liquid through my biggest organ to put stuff on my insides is good for me. I know. I've gotten the explanation about how shots keep you from getting sick. like a million times. It still doesn't seem right to me.

You have to admit, it is a little nuts how you freak out.

Anyway. being with perfect-patient Max makes my fear seem worse and makes me look even more stupid. I am very glad we didn't have to go together. Plus. the last thing I want to do is have a doctor check me over with my brother in the same room. It is embarrassing enough with my mother there.

Mom really can be embarrassing!

I don't think there is anything weird about not liking to go to the doctor. I think it is much, much weirder to love going to the doctor. Just to get attention. And now, I am done writing about the doctor.

We just have

8

more topics to write about!

WOO HOO

Icky Babies By Maggie

Nice title, Maggie!

I think every kid has this kind of day at one time or another. You know, the kind where you get stuck playing with your parent's friend's kids. Welcome to my day. My mom told me yesterday that her old college friend, Ann, is in town this week and she is stopping by.

Look, Maggie! It's super evil zombie baby

and it's going to get you!

Ann is always super nice to us. There is one problem. Ann has a baby. Yep. A baby. Not a lie-there-and-do-nothing kind of baby, but the kind that is still really small, but can walk around. That is the worst kind of baby.

Goo Goo Ga Ga

Waaaah!

I'm not exactly sure why people are made the way they are. I mean, a human baby can walk and move around, but it clearly doesn't have the brain to figure out what the heck it is doing. It seems like it would be safer and less annoying if babies just laid there until they got a little smarter, and then were allowed to move.

This is going to be good. Maggie is deathly afraid of babies. I can't wait to read what she wrote.

I never licked the floor! Only you did that!

My mom is always telling stories about things Max and I did when we were babies. We did A LOT of gross things. Like licking the floor. My mom said she actually had to tell me to stop licking the floor. I was so completely grossed out the first time I heard that. Just hearing the words made my tongue feel all gross and gritty. Like it had just happened.

GROSS!

HA!

I asked her. "Was I hungry? Did I drop some food I was trying to pick up without my hands?" I was looking for some possible explanation as to why I would do something so disgusting. Mom told me that I wasn't hungry. I did not drop any food. I was just exploring. Apparently babies do things like that sometimes. GROSS!

Clearly, I didn't have a brain yet. I just felt like licking the floor for no reason whatsoever. Seriously, I should not have been allowed to move before my brain worked.

Sometimes I wonder if your brain works now... hee hee

I saved room on this page for Max to draw me licking the floor because I know he will.

Thanks, Maggie. This space was perfect for you licking the floor. How thoughtful you are!

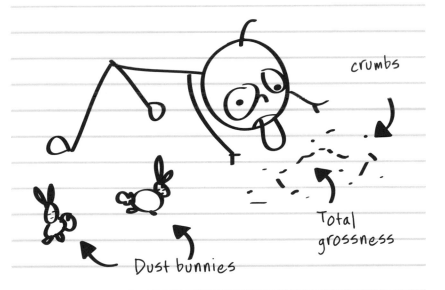

crumbs

Total grossness

Dust bunnies

My mom loves to tell the stories about all of the gross, dumb things we used to do. She actually seems to think that it was all "cute" ????? WHAT????? There are more things, but I can't talk about them. It is seriously too disgusting... ExCEPT...

Max did crazy things too. One time, Max put his foot in the toilet. IN THE TOILET. EW! Really, that is the most un-Max-like thing ever. He's so disgusted by smells and germs and all of that stuff. There is no way he would have done that if he had a ready-to-move brain. Ever.

Max is always drawing disgusting or awful pictures of me, so here is one of Max putting his foot in the toilet. Enjoy, Max!

That's sickening! I did not ever do that and I would not ever do that!

I will leave Max alone now and write about babies in general. Because they are gross. In general.

Besides having an undeveloped brain, another thing about babies is that they are always wet. Their faces are always slobbery. Their hands are wet and sticky from being in their slobbery mouths. I've even seen them suck on their feet, so their socks are all wet, too. And that's a regular, healthy baby that isn't even sick!

If you get a sick one, they are runny and crusty, too. I can't even talk about what happens on the other end without throwing up a little in my mouth. I am aware that I was a gross-sticky baby myself not so long ago, and my mom says I'll grow out of my disgust as I get older, but I have to say, I'm just not sure. Ick.

Runny and crusty? That's disgusting, Mags!

Now you are really grossing me out. I don't know if I can read the rest of this...

100% Icky Baby

Slobbery, slimy, drool-filled mouth (a.k.a. slime producer, screaming machine, favorite place to put things)

Brain: It is actually smaller than a raisin.

Super sneaky, beady eyes

This is actually my hair. Yep. A big old chunk of it.

HA! I wondered if you were going to mention that!

Fat little wobbly and uncoordinated legs

Sticky, slimy, pudgy little fat fingers for grabbing everything. Ew.

Puddle of drool that follows icky baby wherever he or she goes.

Anyway, as you may have guessed, I am not that good with babies. When Max and I meet people who have babies, people automatically assume I would be the better babysitter because I am the girl. Not true.

People sit their baby next to me and tell it to wave its pudgy, wet, sticky hands at me. What they don't know is that Max is the one they should be talking to. I am sitting there just trying to figure out how I'm going to get away from this roly-poly, wet, little person before I get slimed with stickiness to the point that I need a shower to wash off the gunk and goo.   **It's true. Babies love me.**

Max has a thing for babies. He thinks they are cute. He can make them smile. He can make them stop screaming. He can make them laugh, and he actually wants to do all of these things. It is weird, and I can't understand what he's thinking.
Babies are cute. Sure, they are slimy too, but they are cute! At least most of them.

Max is also a real germaphobe. He washes his hands about a hundred times a day. Every day. He's always neat and clean. You'd think he'd be completely disgusted by sticky, germy, leaky babies, but for some reason, he is not.

No I don't! I'm not that bad!

Face it, Mags. You'll never understand me

My mom's friend came over and brought her baby who is 18 months old. I guess that makes me about 128 months old then. Seriously? Who counts ages in months?

Teachers totally do that. Last year, my teacher told us she had a 28-month-old at home. What? I thought she was just trying to trick us into doing some math before I realized that lots of adults actually count a baby's age in months.

When I found out that Mom's friend was bringing a baby, I spent my day moving my stuff around so it didn't get licked or chewed or slobbered on. I guess it wasn't a whole day, but it seemed like a long time. Babies are exhausting.

The good news is that the baby slept almost the whole time she was here. In the short time she was awake, I was able to avoid the stickiness for the most part. She only got me once with her little hands, and it's just because my hair is long, and I couldn't get it out of the way fast enough. I think I handled it well. I didn't "behave rudely", as Mom would say, by running away in fear or looking too disgusted. I am very proud of myself!!!!

Well, good for you, Maggie!

Babies, and Why They Love Me
By Max (the Baby Charmer)

I don't know how you do it. Max.

My mom's best friend from college, Ann, came to visit today. She lives about 8 hours away, so Mom hardly ever gets to see her. Ann is really nice. She was in my parents' wedding, and Mom says she helped out with us a lot when we were babies.

When we were born and Ann still lived close to us, my dad was working really long hours and traveling a lot at his old job. Ann was here all the time helping my mom. Mom calls Ann a lifesaver. I guess it is hard for one person to take care of two babies at the same time, even if they are awesome, like Maggie and me.

Max said I was awesome??!?! That's AmAZING. I am totally framing this!

A few years ago, Ann got married and moved away. We were in the wedding, and of course, we were amazing. People oohed and ahhed, and took our picture when we walked down the aisle. We were pretty cute that day.

Now Ann has a baby. She's in town this week visiting her parents, and my mom is so excited to see her.

I like Ann a lot, but she and my mom drive me crazy when they are together. First, they talk really fast. It's like they are trying to get a year's worth of conversations done in an hour or two. They tell a million and a half stories. They start saying, "Remember when we..." then laugh and laugh. But it's like they (never actually finish a sentence.) I think it's weird to think about Mom being young, too, but some of the stories are probably really funny if I ever got to hear the rest.

This is true! They laugh constantly!!

That drives me crazy!

Of course she brought the baby! Did you think she was going to leave her at home?

Ann brought her baby. Her name is Sammie, and she is a little over a year old. She is really small and completely bald. Really, like, no hair at all. On a girl. But she smiles a lot, and she laughs, and she is totally interested in the weirdest things. She spent forever playing with one of Mom's big kitchen serving spoons. She hit stuff with it, she chewed on it, she sat on it, and then she threw it. It was quite entertaining.

What is even funnier than watching Baby Sammie is watching Maggie try to avoid Baby Sammie!! Maggie is completely afraid of babies. I know, it's ridiculous, right? But she is seriously afraid of them. She acts like she just doesn't like them, but she's totally afraid.

Actually, she's PETRIFIED of a baby. This is how she looks:

whatever!

It's like she can't even stand to touch the baby!
It's hysterical!

I could tell by looking at Maggie that all she wanted to do was run away, but Mom was there, watching. Maggie would be in huge trouble if she was rude to Sammie, and running away from someone's baby is definitely rude.

I know! I was totally stuck!

That is not what I look like!

Maggie was sitting there trying to stay calm, with this absurd look on her face that she thinks is a smile, but is really more of a look like she's going to puke.

Sammie waddled over to her. Maggie tried to casually lean out of the way, but Sammie was too fast. She got a huge chunk of Maggie's hair in her fat little hand, gave it a good yank, and shoved it in her mouth. The look on Maggie's face was priceless. Utter horror.

Ouch! I think I have a bald spot!

HAHAHAHAHAHAHAHAHAHAHAHAHAHAHAHAHA!

HAHAHAHAHAHAHAHAHAHAHAHAHAHAHAHAHAHA!

I laughed so hard I was rolling on the floor. Baby Sammie thought my laughing was funny, too, and she let go of Maggie's hair and laughed and rolled, too. Maggie didn't let Sammie get within 10 feet of her the rest of the day. Luckily, Sammie fell asleep and stayed asleep most of the time. I kept hoping she would wake up again, just so I could see what Maggie would do, but it didn't happen.

Really funny.

The fearless Maggie is 10 years old. She is one of the toughest kids in school, even when you include the boys. She acts like she's not afraid of anything. I think it is absolutely hilarious that a tiny, bald, 20 pound baby scared the heck out of her!!!!

And don't you forget it. Max!

Did you not see my picture a few pages ago?

Who knew that doctors and babies could be so terrifying?!

Let me just say that I am not scared of babies. I dislike them. A lot. There is a BIG difference!

Max's Guide to Babies -
It's really quite simple.

1. Smile.
2. Laugh.
3. Make silly faces.
4. Avoid diapers. (If you smell something, make yourself scarce.)

Yes! Avoid diapers - always!

Maggie's Guide to Babies:

1. Run.
2. Watch out for slobber.
3. Protect your hair.
4. Save your stuff from being licked.
5. Keep fingers away from baby's mouth.
6. If it sneezes, run!

Lucky number 7!

Just 7 more torturous writing tasks left to go.

Thank goodness.

Come on Max, it's not that bad!

Baseball

By Max: Pitcher Extraordinaire

   I love playing baseball, and I love my team. We have lost only one game so far this season. Yep, we're pretty awesome. The only thing that can ruin my happiness is a bunch of arrogant, big-headed travel baseball kids, and that is what I ran into last night.

   Sports are pretty big here - in our suburb. Our town has about 35,000 people (according to my social studies teacher last year). There are a bunch of elementary schools and one gigantic high school, so there are lots of kids, lots of sports, and lots of different teams.

Everyone loves sports and practically everyone plays sports. Except ME. (:

   The high school teams are always going to the state championships for football, baseball, basketball, soccer, etc... They don't always win, but they are usually somehow in championship games. So everyone in our town backs sports. In other words, sports are kind of a big deal.

   Some of us could care less about sports.

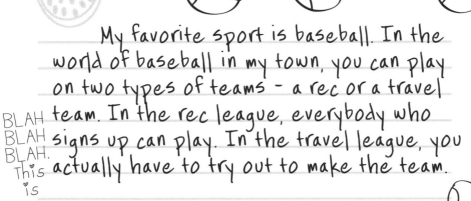

My favorite sport is baseball. In the world of baseball in my town, you can play on two types of teams - a rec or a travel team. In the rec league, everybody who signs up can play. In the travel league, you actually have to try out to make the team.

BLAH BLAH BLAH. This is soooo boring.

The travel teams are usually pretty good. They have full uniforms, matching baseball bags with their names sewn onto them, and they play teams from all over the place. The thing is, they play about 65-85 games each summer! That's a lot of baseball. We only play about 20 games.

I play in the rec league. I played with a group of kids when I was in first grade, and the five of us have played together every summer since. We play really well together, and we have had a great record over the years. Our team is the Tigers and our logo looks like this:

 Not really. More like this...

I'm fine with playing rec. I really love my team. My coach is awesome. The kids are fun. Every once in a while, we get a kid that really doesn't care about baseball, but it's not the end of the world. Plus, I can't imagine playing 85 games. That seems ridiculous.

That is ridiculous! Do you know how much I would hate baseball if I had to go to 85 games?! UGH!

I know a lot of kids that play on the travel teams, and I'm friends with most of them. There is just one team that I can't stand - the Bulldogs.

Yeah, those guys are so rude!

~~Bulldogs~~

The Bulldogs are the elite travel baseball team in our town. The best players are on that team. They practice year-round and they play a few times a week, plus they go out of town to play almost every weekend. Have I mentioned that these players are 11 years old? This is not the pros people, hellooo!

I think the Bulldogs may be more into themselves than Max is into himself! Ha!

I ✗ the Bulldogs!

The Bulldogs are so intense when it comes to baseball, they are totally full of themselves — they think they are hot stuff. I mean, they're good, but not THAT good.

And, just when I thought the players were bad, I watched their parents. They are just as crazy — probably even crazier. The parents are really intense. You can hear them yelling from the stands all the time. The coach yells and stomps around a lot, too. The kids are competitive, the parents are ultra competitive, and the coaches are ridiculously competitive! There's no way I could handle that kind of pressure. Ugh!

Newsflash: Baseball is supposed to be fun!
→ Bummer for you? Bummer

The bummer is that we all play in the same ballpark. There are 8 fields and sometimes, the Bulldogs play in the field right next to us. That's exactly what happened last night.

for me! That place is soooooooo boring!!

I was pitching last night, and I was doing pretty well. As I started the 3rd inning, I had 5 strikeouts and no walks. I was concentrating on warming up, and I heard some familiar voices at the fence. It was 4 of the Bulldogs, all dressed in their fancy uniforms, hanging on the fence, watching me pitch.

Now, I know these guys. There is no way to win at this point. If I pitched really well, they'll tell me that if I was pitching on their team, I'd have gotten smoked. If I stink-ugh, I don't even want to think about what they'd say to me.

I started panicking. It's hard enough to concentrate when you're pitching, but then when you add in those big-headed Bulldogs heckling you from the fence, that is big-time pressure that I did NOT need.

I seriously considered walking off the field and pretending I was sick.

Stop letting those guys get to you, Max. You're just as good as them. Plus, you're nicer!

This is how you looked:

Then, all of a sudden, before the inning actually started, they just left. I couldn't figure out why they'd miss an opportunity to give someone else a hard time. Definitely not like them.

But then, as I looked by the fence again, I understood. Standing along the fence was my sister, looking super impressed with herself as she cheered for me.   You're welcome.

This was unusual, because most of the time, she hates watching my games. She had clearly said something to those guys to get them to leave. I still have to find out what she said to them, but whatever it was, it worked. My sister is a force to be reckoned with. There are quite a few kids at school who are a little scared of her (including me sometimes!).

Who is
scared
of me?   You can thank me later
          for my amazingness.

No I don't!

It's funny, she loves to be mean to me, but she sure has my back if anyone else messes with me. Sometimes, it's a little embarrassing that my sister comes across tougher than me, but sometimes I guess it's a good thing. It is a good thing. Clearly, you are very lucky to have me!

I ended up pitching a 3 up - 3 down inning! I had 2 strikeouts, and one pop-up that I caught easily. Sweet!

See, I told you that you were good!

Final score:

WOO HOO!

Tigers   Falcons

9   5

Well done, Max. I will gladly take partial credit for your victory. I did play an important role, ya know!

Baseball Is ~~Boring~~ Awesome   By Maggie

Max loves baseball.

Baseball in the summer, basketball in the winter. Max loves it. It keeps him busy. All good. That's great. I mean, that's great for Max. For me? Not so much. Because I have to go to every game. Every single one. Ugh!

It's kind of like how I get stuck going to the zoo!

It gets a little old sitting there, a few days a week, watching a bunch of sports that I really have no interest in. I don't understand why I can't stay home by myself. It would be so much more fun at home. It's so boring sometimes. I am not into watching sports - whether it is live or on television.

Sometimes basketball games are not so bad because I know some other kids there. and I can hang out with them. At the high school. there are these big jail-ish walls keeping you from going into some places. but the cafeteria is open. so it's fun to walk around.

Oh, come on! It's not that bad!

But baseball games = not fun. There is absolutely NOTHING around the baseball fields except more and more baseball fields. Tons of them. There are a million cars in the parking lot and people everywhere.

It is super crowded. There are adults playing on some fields and little kids playing on other ones. Girls play softball and they pitch so fast it makes my head spin. It's nuts.

This is what it looks like at the baseball park:

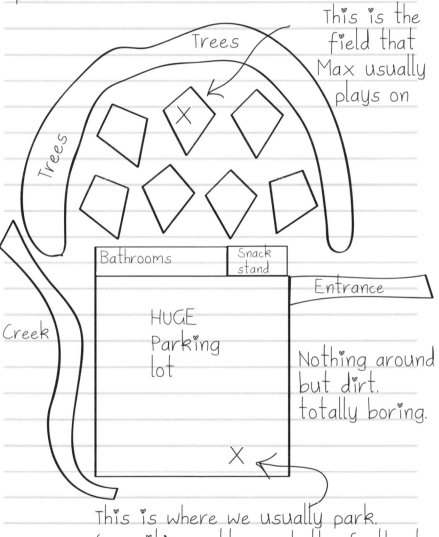

This is the field that Max usually plays on

Trees

Trees

X

Bathrooms

Snack stand

Entrance

Creek

HUGE Parking lot

X

Nothing around but dirt. totally boring.

This is where we usually park. (yep. it's pretty much the farthest spot away from the field.)

well, anyways...

Mom worries too much!

My mom doesn't like for me to wander around too much during Max's baseball games. She gets worried because it's so crowded. I am almost eleven years old, so I think it's a bit ridiculous, but she's not going to change her mind.

Never...

So, baseball is my:
least-favorite-brother-watching activity because I have to just sit there the whole time.

Maggie, you need a hobby!

Also, we have to park so far away. I feel like I've walked a mile by the time we get to the field. It is really, really far to get to the field. Plus, we have to carry these chairs and bags and snacks and water. I feel like one of those mules in the desert carrying stuff. It's a lot of work.

A little workout is good for you!

Then, there's Braden. Braden is the brother of Nick, who's on Max's team. Braden is two or three years older than me, and he DOES NOT STOP TALKING. I mean, he talks ALL the time. Sometimes people say that kind of thing just to be funny, but I mean it. The kid cannot shut his mouth.

He is like the Energizer Bunny -

Oh my gosh!

You're right, Braden is so annoying! I'm glad Nick isn't like that!

he keeps going and going ang going and going and going... Except instead of a drum, he has a mouth.

Whenever I have to go
to a game, I make sure
I always bring
a bag of stuff
to do, like:
drawing pads,
my iPod,
books to read,
my cell phone,
so I can text
my friends
if anyone is around.

At least that stuff
keeps me busy while
I have to sit there.

Sometimes I beg Dad
to let me take his iPad
so I can play games
like Fruit Ninja
and Angry Birds.

Nice
pictures,
Maggie.

LOVE Fruit Ninja!

Braden and Nick's parents are friends with my parents. so we always sit together. The problem is that Braden brings nothing to do. so he bugs me for 2 hours. He reads over my shoulder. he grabs stuff out of my hands. he touches my hair. he steals my snacks...ugh...I could go on and on. Braden is the most annoying human I have ever met. He's right up there at the top of the list with babies.

He's like that annoying kid at the zoo! Ha!

Smart thinking, Mags! Sometimes I pretend I have to go to the bathroom or something. just to get away from Braden for a while. He is actually the reason I was standing by the fence instead of sitting with my parents. He was driving me crazy. so I walked down the first-base fence. and I saw some kids from the Bulldogs. I know Max thinks those guys are big jerks and totally full of themselves. They never bother me too much. but Max can't stand them.

The Bulldogs are HUGE jerks! You're right - I can't stand them!

I could hear them talking about Max.
and it started to make me mad. I could tell
Max was getting worked up. too. and I
didn't like it. I am the only one allowed to
torment my brother. There's no way I am
letting those guys do it. too. Anyway. it
took me less than a minute to get those
guys running back to their field. They are
not very tough. They just have big mouths.

Thanks.
I think

Max thinks the boys at school are
afraid of me just because I don't put up
with their teasing. I don't think they are
actually afraid of me. but they don't like
it that I call them out when they are mean.
Everyone else just tries to ignore them.
I don't care what they think of me (or my
friends). Why should their opinion matter?
It doesn't.

**I don't think they are afraid of you.
I KNOW they are afraid of you!**

You were there for me. Thanks.

I was glad I was there. Max needed me
and I was there for him. He should thank me
later. After all that. Max had a great game
and I even watched a little.

Awwww! You watched? A tear of happiness
is running down my cheek right now!

Maggie's Guide to Watching Sports:

1. Bring lots of stuff to keep yourself entertained.

2. Bring snacks. You could be there for a long time.

3. Never wear sandals to baseball. The dusty, dirty field gets all over your feet and sometimes you get rocks in your sandal and that really hurts.

4. Beg your dad to let you use his computer/iPad/notebook/Kindle.

5. Clap when other people clap so it looks like you are watching. But make sure it's the people on your side clapping. Don't accidentally cheer for the wrong team.   **Yeah. I hate it when you do that!**

6. Watch out for foul balls - they can hit you and that would not be good.

We are halfway done!

ONLY

6

more to go!

Now get ready for
the best topic ever...

By Maggie

Yay! Yay! Yay! Yay! Yay!

Yesterday was a great day. It was one of my favorite days of the summer. It was ICE CREAM DAY!!!

We do this special thing with ice cream every year, and yesterday was the 3rd Annual Pruitt Family Ice Cream Judging Contest.

During the summer, Dad always takes a few days off work. Sometimes he takes days to fix stuff and do projects around the house. (Those days are not good days. Dad hates fixing stuff.)

Ugh. That's the worst!

Then there are always at least two days he takes off just for us to do fun stuff, including ICE CREAM Day.

Understatement of the year. You eat more ice cream than anyone I know....

Ice Cream Day is my favorite day of the year because I love ice cream. I mean LOVE it! I eat ice cream more than any other food. Really. My favorite flavors are chocolate and mint chocolate chip at home, but if we go to an ice cream stand, cake batter is the best. In a giant waffle cone. That is bigger than my whole head. Delicious.

You DO eat ice cream every day!

I could eat ice cream every day if Mom and Dad let me. I'd make a gigantic bowl of it because cones are too complicated at home. I could eat a whole gallon by myself. That's true, but totally gross

Lucky for me, my dad loves ice cream, too. He and I went out one night and had an ice cream tour. We stopped at 4 different ice cream stands and had a cone at each one. I was pretty stuffed afterward, but it was totally worth it. Mom and Max like ice cream. (I mean, who doesn't) but not like Dad and me. No one in the enire world likes ice cream like you and Dad.

Sometimes I imagine that I live in a city where there are ice cream rivers and hot fudge waterfalls...and I would travel in a boat with spoons for oars so I could eat ice cream whenever I want! That would be the best! It would be a dream come true!

That sounds sticky and gross. Like baby goo.

This was totally my idea — because I ROCK!!! But you are only supposed to have a taste of each kind, not the whole container....

A few years ago, we started having this huge ice cream judging contest. We pick a flavor, gather samples of that flavor from a bunch of different places, then come home and taste and judge. We vote for our favorites and we pick a winner each year.

We pick a day in the middle of the summer. Dad takes the day off work. We start first thing in the morning. Mom gets out two big coolers and puts a bunch of those frozen, blue ice packs in them. We load the coolers in the back of the car and head out on our ice cream quest.

The quest is the best part!

We pick one flavor of ice cream to collect. The first year, we did vanilla, the second year, mint chocolate chip, and this year it's CHOCOLATE!! Yay!

Then we spend about three hours driving from store to store, buying every brand of our flavor of the day from each store. We stop at grocery stores, convenience stores, drug stores - any place we can find that sells ice cream.

You forgot the to-go containers at the actual ice cream stores.

After each stop, we put the ice cream in the coolers until they are both full. Then we take the ice cream home and have a big ice cream judging contest.

Dad prints a list of all the different brands while Mom super-secretly labels bowls with the name of the ice cream and puts a scoop or two in each bowl. Then we taste and give each bowl a rating from 1-10 (10 being the most delicious).

Although Grandma totally peeked when she judged with us last year...

After we are finished, Mom puts all of our numbers on a spreadsheet, and we figure out the best brand of ice cream. I don't think she knows what SUPER-SECRET means... ←

This is a very serious competition.

It's a pretty serious competition. Dad and I look forward to it every year. Dad always says we should eat nothing but ice cream that WHOLE DAY. but Mom always makes us eat real food. too.

I look forward to it too!

Thank goodness.

We spent all day yesterday on our competition. It was great. We laughed and laughed. and got very full on ice cream. At one point. I laughed so hard. ice cream almost shot out of my nose!

Yes, it was!

Turns out. the best chocolate ice cream was Spicer Dairy Chocolate. I've never had it before. but it was delicious. I hope Mom remembers where we bought it so we can get more. Of course. that won't be necessary for a while. because the whole freezer is packed with leftover ice cream. Yum!

↓ The last thing I want to see is you throwing up!

I totally picked the winner.

Ice Cream Day By Max (the Stuffed)

I am really not sure how my dad and my sister can eat so much ice cream. My dad is a full-sized adult, but Maggie is pretty little. She's one of the smallest kids in our class, but, man, can she eat a lot of ice cream. *Because it's delicious!*

The ice cream competition was fun. I like the tradition of it. We make a big deal out of picking all of the brands, Dad makes spreadsheets on the computer to tally the scores. It's very fun. We laugh a lot and joke, and drink water in between tastes of ice cream to cleanse our palettes. It's all good, but after the competition, I am done with ice cream. Seriously done.

Bottomless pit in Maggie's stomach

I can't believe Maggie and my dad don't get sick of ice cream after that. Mom and I don't touch the stuff for at least a month after the competition. We just get sick of it. Not Dad OR Maggie - they are like bottomless ice cream pits.

My dad is kind of like a kid sometimes.
I mean, he goes to work every day and does
grown-up stuff, but he really likes to fool
around, and he likes to break the rules, too.
I am a lot like him — unless it comes to
eating my body weight in ice cream, then
Maggie is more like him.

No kidding!

Dad is the best.
He is so funny!

He loves ice cream so much and he
loves a good competition. That may be why he
had an ice cream eating competition one day
with a guy from work. Really. Two grown men.
My dad is hilarious.

This story is so funny!

I know, right?

Here is the **TRUE** story: After lunch
one day, my dad and his buddy from work
stopped at a local ice cream place. This ice
cream place has something on its menu called
"The Stuffer." The Stuffer is ridiculous. It
starts with a big aluminum container that
is so big it can hold like 5 jugs of milk. You
get 9 scoops of ice cream, three toppings, a
banana and a whole bunch of whipped cream
on top.

The Stuffer

sprinkles

whipped cream

mint chocolate chip

pecan

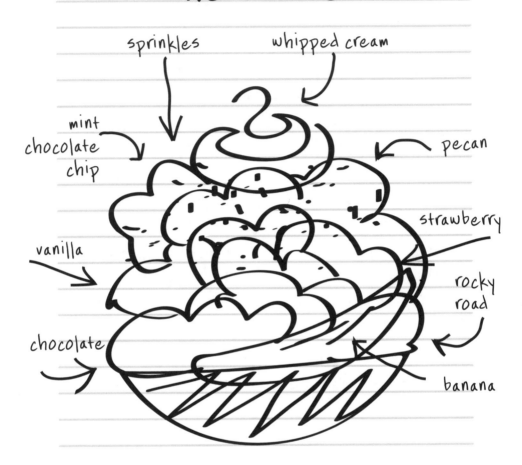

vanilla

strawberry

rocky road

chocolate

banana

My dad claimed he could eat that much ice cream, but his friend didn't believe him.

Challenge Accepted.
Oh yeah! Dad loves a challenge!

Sure enough, a few days later, my dad and his work buddies went to the ice cream place after lunch and my dad ordered The Stuffer. Now, my dad isn't a big guy, and he usually doesn't eat that much, but ice cream is the exception. I bet Dad could eat MORE than his weight in ice cream.

His friends bet him $20 that he couldn't eat the whole thing. He took the bet. Of course he ate the whole thing. Then he drank the melty-gunk at the bottom of the dish, just to prove he could. Clearly, he won the bet. Then he went and threw up in the bathroom. Regardless, he won the bet, and he still loves ice cream. My dad is never boring.

Dad never turns down a bet.

Yeah. I don't eat that melty gunk. That's nasty.

Never - that's for sure!!

Max's Guide to Eating Ice Cream –

1. Choose a flavor like vanilla, chocolate or mint chocolate chip. The other flavors are disgusting.

2. Order a normal-sized cone.

Ice cream is NEVER disgusting!

3. Enjoy.

4. Don't eat ice cream again for a few days at least.

A little ice cream = good

9 scoops = ~~BAD~~ Better

(:

We are almost there!

Just

more writing assignments left to go! The end is in sight.

Hotels By Max (the Cool)

Last week we had our annual family ice cream contest, and this week we're going with Dad on an overnight business trip. He has a meeting about 3 hours away, and he has one more meeting the next day. Mom just finished a big project for work and she has a few days off, so we decided to go with him. Mom and Maggie and I will find something to do while Dad's working, then we get to stay overnight in a hotel. Maybe there's a zoo close- by! (:

I love staying overnight in a hotel.

Me too!

It's so much fun, especially if there is a pool. I love it when they have room service, where they bring your breakfast right to your room on a big rolling cart. It's like breakfast in bed. I love room service. It is awesome. It makes you feel like you are rich or something.

Room service is the best. When we are allowed to get it!

Plus, Mom and Dad always let us go fill the ice bucket and explore the different parts of the hotel. Sometimes they give us money for the pop machine or the candy machine so we can get snacks. I love those little caramels with the white stuff inside. So good. You like those caramel things??
Ew. Gross.

We ride the elevator and check out the weight room or the breakfast area and the gift shop. It's fun to wander. Maggie and I actually get along great when we are wandering. It's like we're on a secret mission together or something.

It's true. We do get along when we are roaming the hotel. Hmmm...

The only bad part about staying in a hotel is having to share a bed with my sister. Most hotel rooms have 2 beds. Well, when we are at a hotel, Maggie and I have to share a bed. That is no picnic.

Sharing with you is no picnic either.

I know! We do have to share EVERYTHING. UGH. Even this journal!

Now, I realize that we are twins. We have spent our whole lives sharing stuff, from even before we were actually born. We share our stuff, we share friends, we share our birthdays. Lots of times, we don't even get our own birthday gifts. We have to share our gifts. Seriously?

I hate sharing gifts!

We shared a room until about 3 years ago, when we both decided we wanted our own space. So after 10 years of sharing, you'd think we could deal with each other for one night in a hotel. Sadly, we cannot.

I can! You are just impossible.

It typically goes like this. We have a fun day, then as soon as it gets dark, Mom and Dad are tired but Maggie and I are still pumped up from a fun day. They say they want to sleep, but we can watch TV or read for a while, until we are tired.

Reading is better. because it makes your eyes tired at night. Maybe you should try it sometime. Max.

Most of the time, I want to turn off the light and play my iPod. I have some books I listen to at night that help me fall asleep. My brain sometimes goes crazy when I am trying to fall asleep, and I can't make it stop thinking. When I listen to a book, it distracts my brain so I can relax and sleep. I don't know why it works, but it does. I just relax and enjoy some stranger reading me to sleep. The stranger part may sound a little weird, but, whatever. It works.

What brain? Just kidding. hee hee.

That is weird.

Maggie, of course, likes to read before she falls asleep. I don't understand how that works, because you have to close your eyes to sleep, and you have to OPEN your eyes to read. It doesn't seem like the two go together. Anyway, Maggie wants to keep the light on and read.

Um. every other person in the whole world can understand this. Except you.

ugggggh!

How exactly am I supposed to fall asleep with a bright light shining in my face?
It looks like this.....

For some reason, my parents can fall asleep almost immediately, so they don't notice the eye-burning, bright light, but I notice it, and there is no way I can sleep like that.

The light is BLINDING!

Yeah. Kinda hard to relax and fall asleep when you are blinded.

Usually, a small disagreement takes place. Mom or Dad yells from their bed that they are tired, and we should work it out. Surprisingly, we don't let it go, and we keep arguing because the light is still on and I still can't sleep.

Another thing about sharing a bed with Maggie is that she smothers us with so many blankets that I think I'm going to die of heat. We push and poke each other, and maybe a kick here and there...until finally, Dad gets mad, gets up and turns off the light and yells at us to go to sleep.

You kick and push me- I am totally innocent here.

It doesn't end there. Maggie and I are lying there in the dark, trying to go to sleep. She thinks you have to lie perfectly still to fall asleep. I need to move around until I get comfortable. After a few minutes, Maggie starts whining at me to stay still. Then she pushes and whisper-yells at me. I shush her and warn her we are going to get in trouble. You move around SO much. it's like sleeping next to a kangaroo!

This whole process repeats until finally, Mom or Dad wakes up and yells at us a while, then we switch places so Dad ends up sharing one bed with me and Mom shares with Maggie. Then, finally, we all go to sleep. HMMMMMM.

When I write about what actually happens when we stay at a hotel, it does make me wonder why I like hotels. Weird. I guess it's only the sharing a bed with Maggie that I don't like.

The sleeping part is the only bad part about the hotel.

Honestly, now that I think about it, I wonder why my parents even try to make us share first. Wouldn't it be easier if we just started the night boys on one side, girls on the other? You know how it is, sometimes parents never learn.

You are totally right. They should let us run the show. Everything would be soooooooooo much easier.

Hotels By Maggie

I love hotels for all the reasons that Max wrote about = the exploring, the vending machines, the room service, the pool. Don't get me wrong, I enjoy traveling and staying in a hotel. However, staying in the same room with Max is impossible. Furthermore, staying in the same bed is absolutely impossible. I mean, REALLY IMPOSSIBLE.

Agree!

I don't know how anyone can sleep near him. He complains about the blankets being too hot and moves around so much the bed shakes.

When we were little, we shared a room. A lot of times, we would stay in the same bed. I don't know how I did it. I'm not sure if he was less difficult then or if I was so used to his craziness that I didn't notice or if I was just so little and didn't know to complain about him yet. Anyway, he's super ~~annoying~~.
Awesome.

You're lucky I don't stink like a penguin.

First of all, Max is a penguin. I mean, the guy likes to be freezing cold when he sleeps. I mean, freezing cold. He has 2 fans in his room. One that hangs on the ceiling and another one that sits on a stand and sprays cold air all over him while he sleeps. It is FREEZING in there at night. We have air conditioning in our house, but it's never cold enough for Max. I am seriously afraid he may freeze to death one night, with a big smile on his face because he's happy to be frozen.

My fans are the best.

They are awesome.

Seriously?!

Not me. I end up like a giant ice cube in the bed, even with a million covers. Brrrrrr!

I cannot sleep like that!

_Ha!_

Plus, he cannot lie still. Max flips and flops and jiggles and wiggles and kicks, and basically, just makes the whole bed feel like a trampoline when you are trying to sleep. It is not possible to sleep in that environment.

I never jiggle!

Ha! NICE!

Then there's the whole reading thing. Reading before you fall asleep is a normal thing to do. Lots of people relax by reading before they fall asleep. Reading makes your eyes tired, so when you put down your book and turn off the light, you are so tired you fall right to sleep.

I disagree. It is NOT that easy.

I sleep just fine, thank you very much.

Maybe Max should try reading sometimes, so he doesn't flip around like a porpoise every night for hours before he actually falls asleep. I don't mean listening to a story on the iPod either. I mean actually reading a book. I'll have to suggest that to Max.
(Or maybe he will actually read this!)

Thank you for the suggestion. I choose to ignore it.

I will never like reading like you and Mom.

I guess I do have to agree with Max. that I don't understand why Mom and Dad even try to make us share a bed. It is hopeless.

See - I am brilliant.
Want a fabulous idea?
Need a problem solved?
Call MAX!!

The good news about this trip is that I think Mom, Max, and I are going to a new zoo while Dad is at his meeting. We have an annual pass to our zoo, and if you have that, you get to go to a bunch of other zoos in different places for free!!! Yay!! That will be awesome. Can't wait!

Wait. Don't I get a say about where we go? I'll have to find a gas mask... (:

Maggie's and Max's Guide to Hotels:

1. Find the ice maker. It is important to get ice in an ice bucket. For no reason at all as far as we can tell, but you must get ice.   *I know, right? Why ice?*

2. Order room service. It is the best.
   Especially breakfast in bed

3. Follow the smell of chlorine to find the pool. Swim, swim, swim.   *Don't forget the hot tub if they have one.*

4. Look for a game room. *Hope for a claw game. Or at least air hockey.*

5. Check the lobby for snacks. Some hotels have cookies, fruit or mints in the lobby.
   Yes!

6. Play with the chain locks. *And check the fire escape plan from your room.*

7. Look through the peep hole at people walking past in the hall. *And say, "Pssst." They won't know where the noise came from!*

8. Save the bottles from the tiny shampoo for potions!   *And to hold ammo.*

10, 9, 8, 7, 6, 5

The end is near! Only 4 more to go.

But that also means the summer is more than halfway over.   :(

We went to Cedar Lakes yesterday. It is my FAVORITE, FAVORITE, FAVORITE amusement park. We had so much fun. We do this every year. Dad takes a day off work, because the parks are less crowded during the week. If you go on Saturday or Sunday, sometimes you have to wait in line more than you get to do anything fun.

Me in line

Anyway,

I LOVE ROLLER COASTERS.

Roller coasters are awesome. Cedar Lakes has the best roller coasters ever. There are seven of them. Two are the older kind. which are made of wood. They are fun. but very bumpy. They shake up your head and make you feel like you are going to fly right out of your seat.

If you want your brain shaken into a milkshake, ride one of those.

Can you say, "Death trap"?"

One of the roller coasters has two tracks. and two trains race each other. On another coaster. you have to stand up during the whole ride.

That one is awesome!

There is also one where you go upside down 4 times. My favorite is the one where you kind of hang underneath the track and dangle below the car. and your feet hang out. That one is really cool. You feel like you are flying.

Also awesome!

I like that one because you are strapped in — shoulders and everything.

The biggest, scariest coaster they have is the Dragon. It is really high and really fast. There is a countdown at the beginning, and when it gets to zero, you get shot forward super fast, and you go straight up this crazy-high track and come STRAIGHT DOWN the other side. It is very short and it may not seem very exciting, but it is so fast and high and steep that it is awesome!

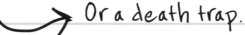 Or a death trap.

The Dragon:

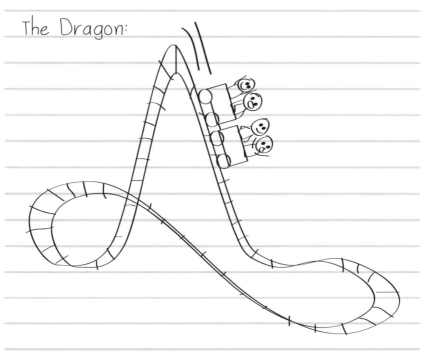

I went on every coaster in the park, EXCEPT for the Dragon. Guess why I didn't go on that coaster? Let me give you a hint: it was not me who was afraid. My ENTIRE FAMILY chickened out on me. All of them.

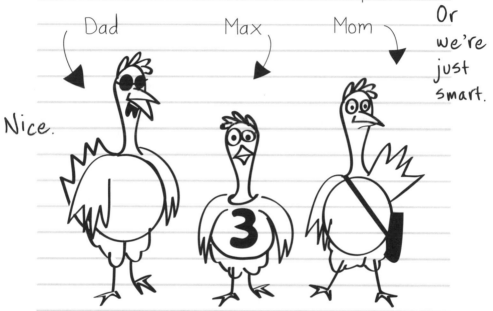

Dad   Max   Mom

Or we're just smart.

Nice.

I kind of expected my mom and Max to chicken out, but my DAD? I am so disappointed in him. I couldn't get anyone to go with me, and my parents wouldn't let me go by myself. So for another year, I missed what appears to be the best ride ever.

At least you are still alive!
We might have saved your life, you know.

Yes it is.

On the bright side, the other coasters were super cool and the junk food is delicious at that amusement park. Oh, the junk! Most delicious item of the day: ice cream, of course. This wasn't just any ice cream though. Today we had ice cream that was not hard ice cream,

Ice cream? not soft ice cream, but instead - a bowl of tiny, little, mini ice cream balls. Well

Really? Surprise, surprise.

I have to say, I wasn't sure how I felt about it at first because it was weird to see ice cream that way, but WOW!!! It was awesome. I don't know who figured out that ice cream is extra good when it is frozen into:

tiny little balls of deliciousness,

but thank you, whoever you are. You have made my life SOOOOOO much better.

YUM.

You are weird, Mags.

I've got to admit, that ice cream was pretty good.

Yes!

We always spend a lot of time in the (arcade.) My father is like a kid when it comes to arcade games. Well, he's like a kid a lot of the time, but especially in arcades. We actually have a full-sized Skee ball game in our basement. That is how super-serious my dad is about arcade games.

This is just one of the reasons Dad is so cool...

My dad and Max also have this super-serious claw game competition going on. I am not sure who is winning now, but they both came home with a pile of stuffed animals. I am not a fan of the competition.

I AM WINNING! I'm beating Dad by 2 grabs!!!

Why?

Because before this, Dad used to give me all the cool (and sometimes weird) stuff he won from the claw game. Whatever he got, he would give to me. What Dad wouldn't want to give his winnings to his sweet, lovable daughter? I love getting that kind of stuff.

Really?

⮕ No kidding.

But now, because of this ~~stupid~~ Amazing competition, I am completely forgotten, and all the stuff he wins goes on some untouchable trophy wall in the basement. Yes, most people put actual trophies on shelves to display. Not at our house. Dad and Max have this shelf that is full of cheap stuffed animals, fake gold watches, basketballs — all kinds of things that they have won over the last year or so. It's really weird.

What is the point of getting a toy if you can't touch it?
I will never understand boys.

Coolest Trophy Wall EVER

You have to be awesome to understand the thrill of competition!!

Cedar Lakes
By Max (the Claw Game Champion)

The best part of going to Cedar Lakes is that I pulled ahead of my dad in the Claw Game Competition. I am now winning 19 to 17. I got a weird heart stuffed animal, a little clear box with a fake diamond ring in it, AND a strange headband that has glowing devil horns on it.

All of which you should have given to your adorable sister.

I got 3 things yesterday, and Dad only got one. The only reason he actually got one was because on my last grab, I loosened up a green alien guy, so Dad had an easy grab on his next turn. Big deal.

I'm totally going to tell Dad you took credit for his win...

This is what my trophy wall will look like — when I add the devil horns, diamond, and heart man, of course.

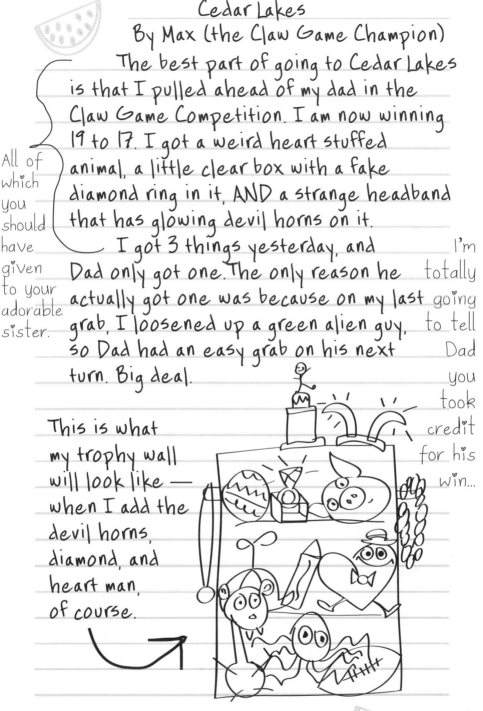

Right now, I'm winning and that's all that matters. This means I can rub it in. I will now send my dad texts as much as possible over the next few days (when he's at work). I will pretty much torment him with the fact that I am beating him.

Guys just love to give each other grief. It's fun. You give it, you take it, and it makes life more interesting.

Max = Winner!

Boys are weird. Even adult boys.

#1

Claw Game Champion

Really?

In my head right now, I can hear the song "We Are the Champions" playing. I may have to get that song ready to play on my iPod when Dad gets home from work, and maybe I'll strut around, holding my head high and patting myself on the back. That would be hilarious. Maybe I'll even wear the devil horns for effect. That is awesome.

Nice.
Max.

Who is the weird one now. Max?

The bad part about our trip to Cedar Lakes yesterday is that Maggie is still bugging me about which rides I will and will not go on at the park. I like rides. They are fun. I love the spinning rides that make you dizzy. I love the high rides that swing you around, and I like the roller coasters — almost all of the roller coasters.

Basic benefit of being a twin: having a built-in person to do stuff with. FYI - You are not holding up your end of the bargain.

My sister keeps bugging me about the fact that there are a few roller coasters I refuse to ride. Not because they are too high or too fast. Actually, the higher and faster the better. My problem is that I do not feel comfortable when I am on a roller coaster that is hurtling me through the air at very high speeds, and the only thing keeping me from being thrown to a very unpleasant death is a tiny little bar across my lap. It just doesn't seem safe.

Me: unintentionally airborne

This is just silly. Millions of people ride these rides EVERY DAY. and nothing like that ever happens!!! EVER. EVER. EVER.

I love the big coasters that have the giant shoulder pad things that come over your head and hold your whole body down during the ride. Bring them on. The more twists and turns and loops there are, the better. I won't be falling out of those.

On the other hand, those little coasters that have a seat belt that's flimsier than the seatbelt in the car — really?

How is that OK with anyone?

Ummm- It's ok with every other person in the whole world.

You feel like you are lifted 3 feet above your seat every time you go over a hill! That's the best part!
I hate those, and I can't understand how other people do not see the problem with them. It's not my fault I have a brain that actually works and wants to keep me alive until adulthood.

You have a brain? hee hee

Other than the death rides we had a great time. I love when Dad is with us all day, and I am not outnumbered by girls. The only other bad thing about going to Cedar Lakes... is it means summer is almost over. We always squeeze a bunch of fun stuff in before school starts, which means that soon 5th grade will start. Ugh.

Nooooooooooooooooooooooo!

They are safer than riding in a car. Max

Max's Guide to Amusement Parks -

1. Eat elephant ears, funnel cakes, and all the other snacks you can only get at parks and fairs and stuff.

ooooooooooh. yeah!

2. Ride safe rides.   They are all safe. you goofball!

3. Avoid death-trap rides.
There are no rides like that!

4. Play the claw game at the arcade.
You are truly obsessed with the claw game.

9 down and only 3 to go!

I'm starting to feel a little sad
about the whole thing ending.
What's this, a tear in my eye?
The sadness is setting in...

Max - you
are nuts!

Grandparents & Stuff by Max
(the Incredible Builder)

My grandparents came over last night. I love when they visit. Grandparents are the best. They totally spoil their grandchildren. At least mine do. Plus, you can hardly ever do anything wrong around them. Stuff that makes my mom mad just makes them laugh. I love that! So that's good.

I ♥☺ Grandma and Grandpa!

Yeah!

Also, my grandma loves to get us stuff. Every time they visit, they bring us our favorite snacks, cool things they found when they were shopping, or some kind of present. My grandpa loves to make cool shooting things with me, and he always brings me more supplies.

Yes she does!

CHOCOLATE!

Paper clips? Now that's boring.

So today I have a big box of awesome things to make. The items may sound weird, but I can make awesome stuff with these things. I've got paperclips, rubber bands, toothpicks, pushpins, little army guys, tape, those black clips that are for holding paper but make great catapults, and a wooden box. Great. You can make more stuff to shoot at me...):

I made the coolest things today. I created this awesome catapult that can shoot almost anything across the whole house. I tried a lot of different things for ammo. Oh. great. Plastic blocks worked pretty well, but they were a little light, so they didn't fly very far. I used a couple of army guys. Those guys Great. worked pretty well. One army guy flying Now I through the air can take down about have to 40 army guys set up about 20 feet away. duck

every
time
     I was perfectly happy setting up   I walk
guys and knocking them over.   into a
room
so I
don't
get hit
with
The Catapult of Awesomeness: some
flying
object.
I feel
safe.

Brilliant?
Really?

Then I had the brilliant idea of shooting some of those rubber bouncy balls — you know, those colorful, super-bouncy powerballs. It seemed like a good idea at the time. They are nice and heavy and round so they fit in my catapult nicely. I was thinking I could really get some distance with these.

How about now?

Well, I was right. I definitely got some distance. Maybe a little more distance than I needed. My first shot went way past my army guy target and flew into the kitchen. It bounced against the wall in the kitchen, and bounced all over the place. It knocked a bunch of stuff off the counter. Mom was not happy with me. There was a lot of chaos - from one little bouncy ball. Who knew?

You almost hit Grandma!

Everyone but you knew what would happen.

When I finished getting in trouble, I looked all over the kitchen for my bouncy ball. No matter what my mom said, it was clearly the best ammo I found, so I really wanted to keep it. I could not find it anywhere. Finally, I just quit looking, and kept working on my contraptions.

Grandpa thought it was funny!

Well, later on I figured out where it went. After we had a nice dinner with Grandma and Grandpa, they went home, and Dad and Mom started cleaning up the kitchen. Mom was washing the dishes, and had all of this really disgusting food stuff and dirty water in the sink, so she started the garbage disposal and it made the terrible noise. Then it groaned for a while and then stopped working completely. UH-OH!

Let me tell you, if there is one thing my dad really does not like, it is fixing stuff around the house. What's even worse, is when he has to touch gross things while he is fixing something.

HA!
TRUE.
That is one of the few things that makes Dad angry.

My dad was not happy messing with the sink to fix the disposal. He had to put his hand in the disgusting stuff, and I'm pretty sure I heard him almost throw up a couple of times. That's when I ran away. I was pretty sure my room was a much safer place to be.

Guess what?

After digging around in the disgusting stuff for a really long time, he found my bouncy ball. Oops. I'm not sure it will make good ammo anymore. I guess those things are not made to survive garbage disposals. It was pretty mangled.

Powerball Before: Powerball After:

What's Awesome About
Grandparents:

1. They buy you your favorite snacks!
   CHOCOLATE! For me - potato chips!   That is the best!

2. They bring you the perfect presents on random days that aren't your birthday.

3. They are hardly ever annoyed by you, and for some reason they don't annoy you either.   Come to think of it, you're right. They have never annoyed me.

4. They are genuinely interested in hearing every detail about what you do all day.   I can't believe it but you are right again!

5. They always have time to do things with you.

   They have like 80 years of great ideas!
6. They have great ideas (like the shoe thing)

Don't forget this though -
Warning: Never wake a napping Grandpa

Grandparents and Stuff By Maggie

Max can make some really cool things. He can turn almost anything into some *Yes I can.* kind of shooting device. One time he took apart a pen and, I have no idea how he did it, but he made something that was like a sling-shot-bow-and-arrow kind *Did you know pens have springs inside?* of thing. It was very cool, but I spent the next week of my life avoiding flying objects that were shot all over the house.

I'm not surprised at all that *Because I make the* Max managed to break something *coolest stuff.* with one of the things he shoots around. Sometimes I feel like I am walking through a battlefield. I don't even know how he comes up with all of this stuff, but I do know that it is not safe to walk around the house unprepared when Max has a box of new stuff.

Me

Random flying objects

I love when Grandma and Grandpa come, but now, since they brought him all kinds of office supplies, he can turn them into weapons. I have to hide in my room a lot today. **Don't hide. Come out. I love a moving target!!! BWAH HAHAHAHA!**

Luckily, they brought me stuff, too. Grandma and Grandpa always find me the best stuff. The first is chocolate. Yum Yum Yum! They bring me chocolate every time they visit. It is the most delicious chocolate, the kind that Mom NEVER buys because she thinks I eat too much ice cream and don't need anymore junk food. I love it! Sometimes they get the ones that have caramel inside and they are so so so so yummy.

Oh yeah, me too!

I get candy that comes in a plastic box. Then I can use the box for my creations!!!

Dark chocolate drizzle

Regular yummy chocolate

Oozing gooey caramel So good!

Then I got this big blue case. I didn't know what it was at first. It was covered with pockets and zippers, and the top opened up and it looked like it held lots of stuff. It had zippers and several pockets and a drawer. It had a sticker with my name on it, too! It looked like this:

Maggie

Well, when I first opened it up I was confused. There was a bunch of stuff in there, but on the top were two pairs of shoes. They were plain white tennis shoes. I was thinking that shoes are kind of a weird gift for someone my age, especially plain white boring shoes. I never wear plain boring stuff. Of course, I smiled and said thanks anyway.

Yay. Shoes. (Can you tell I am being sarcastic?)

You make Mom proud!!

Grandma laughed, because she probably knew what I was thinking. Then she explained. The blue box was full of all kind of things I could use to decorate the shoes. It had fabric markers, fabric paint, a little tool to make tiny gems stick to fabric, some clear glittery spray to make them sparkle, and a bunch of cool ribbons to use as shoelaces.

GIRLY stuff. Yuck.

Oh. Now I am excited. I usually get in trouble when I draw on my shoes. Sometimes when school gets boring, I doodle on my shoes. Mom does not like that one bit. She says I am ruining them! But it's funny — Grandma actually wants me to draw on shoes!!

BORING. My stuff is way cooler.

That is exactly what I am going to do this afternoon. I only have 2 pairs of shoes, so I really have to think about how I want to decorate them. It's great, because I can wear them on the first day of school, which is coming very soon. Everybody will love them. It will be awesome.

Aaaaaaaaaaagh! Don't talk about school!

My ^super awesome shoes!

Those are actually pretty cool, Mags!

We are SO close!
There are just:

2

♡journal entries left!

Back to School By Maggie

Well, it is coming. I know it. I'm try-ing to pretend it's not, but every time we leave the house, there are reminders everywhere. Back to school. **Noooooooooooo** BLAAAAHHHHH.

No place is safe! Not even a grocery store!

The first time I noticed was at the grocery store. Now, most people would thing a grocery store would be safe from back-to-school stuff. After all, there are not really many groceries involved in going back to school. Maybe snacks and stuff for your lunchbox, but that is pretty much it. But for some crazy reason, the whole front of the grocery store was packed with back-to-school stuff. I don't get it. why would a grocery store sell backpacks, pencils, paper and all of that stuff? A grocery store should be a safe place for a kid to go in August without being reminded that it is almost time to go back to school.

We may have to stay home to save ourselves!

Glue

10 days!?!?! ugh!

We only have 10 days left before the end of summer break. I can't believe it. The summer went really fast. I guess the non-school days always go faster than school days. Well, that may not be true. Sometimes it gets boring being home, especially because we don't have any neighbors to hang out with. It's really just been me and Max, pretty much the whole summer. I am excited to see some of my friends again. That will be fun.

The LONGEST days are when you are boring and won't do anything with me all day!

HEY! The Pruitts are never boring!

The other thing about school starting: It means we get to go out and buy new school clothes, which is usually fun, unless, of course, Max comes with us.

Just say NO to SHOPPING!

I hope Mom lets me get the GIGANTIC box of crayons this year, you know, the one with the sharpener on the back of the box. That would be: AWESOME!

· Summer ·

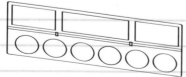

It is pure torture!

Max hates shopping for clothes. I mean, he really hates it. He's not so bad when we just pick something out quick, but if we take longer than a few minutes or if we make him wait while we try stuff on, it is a disaster. At first, he just grunts and grumbles. Then he throws himself down on the nearest chair or floor, and moans and groans. People passing by think he's sick or dying or something. Maybe Max should have a little more patience.

I have not thrown myself on the ground in years.

When we were little, he got so mad about shopping with us that he hid in the middle of one of the clothes racks. It really is like a cave in the middle of those round racks, you know, with a big round wall of clothes surrounding you. Mom kept calling for him, over and over, and over again, and he didn't answer because he was angry. Everyone in the store was looking for him. Mom was mad at first, but then she started crying because she was worried. There were tons of people looking for him everywhere.

I had to get away from you two crazy shoppers!

Before long, I found him. Luckily, I was pretty short at the time, so I could see stuff down low that all of the grown-ups missed. I was walking around mostly confused, but getting a little scared because Mom was so upset, and then I spotted his little legs. I stuck my head into the clothes rack, and there he was.

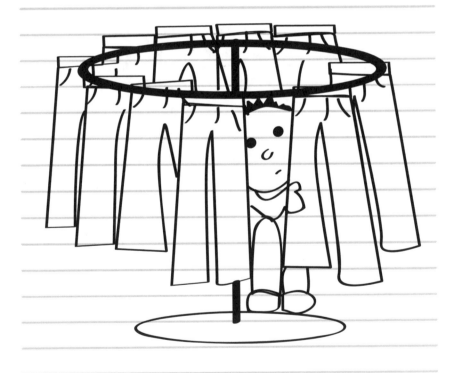

I yelled for mom, and she came running. She hugged Max and kept crying. Max didn't even get in trouble because Mom was so happy to find him.

I still don't know why she was crying. I was fine.

Anyway, that's the kind of stuff that happens when Max has to go shopping with us. Mom and I love to get clothes. We could shop and shop and shop. We have to try stuff on, or else we end up with clothes that feel yucky. That is no good.

Maggie + Clothes = true LOVE

Sometimes Mom buys us clothes when she's out by herself. I always tell the truth if I don't like something, because she'll return it and I won't get stuck wearing it. But if I choose to keep it, I have to wear it. It really bugs Mom if she buys clothes that we don't wear. She says it's a big waste of money.

Once in a while, I end up getting something that just doesn't feel right later at home or after it's washed. I have to wear it anyway. Sometimes clothes become so uncomfortable to wear. Once I got a pair of jeans that fit pretty well, except they had this gigantic gap at the waist. I am not sure who fits into jeans that are shaped like that, except maybe someone with a turtle shell for a back. I hate that!

Is that a disco turtle, Mags?

If so, you are weird.

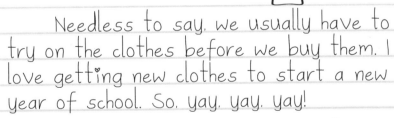

Needless to say, we usually have to try on the clothes before we buy them. I love getting new clothes to start a new year of school. So, yay, yay, yay!

Mom and I will definitely be shopping soon. I can't wait. Hopefully, Max can stay home with Dad and we'll just bring stuff home for him. He doesn't seem to care what kind of clothes we get him. He'll wear pretty much anything.

I can't believe you are happy about this. Do you understand that SCHOOL is STARTING SOON?!?!?!?

I must start planning my wardrobe. Soon it will be the first day of school again. What shall I wear? Hmmm...

Seriously? You are nuts!

This is Maggie and her clothes

Back to School   By Max
(The One Who Is NOT Ready to Go Back)

OK, two things here:
1. Maggie is right that it is almost time for school to start again.

2. Maggie is completely wrong that shopping for clothes is the best part of back to school.

I didn't say it was the best part.

Maggie actually seems kind of excited about going back to school. I am not excited at all. Maggie can't wait because she gets new stuff and she gets to see all of our friends again, and all of that kind of stuff. Sure, I like that part, too.

No. I am excited about getting new stuff. Max. NOT about school. I'm not that crazy!

The thing Maggie doesn't seem to realize is that with school comes work. Homework. Tests. Studying. Reports. And pressure. It doesn't bother Maggie, because she doesn't care if she gets good grades.

YES I do!

However, I do. I care about grades. I can't help it. I don't want to care so much. Sometimes I wish I could be like Maggie and not worry about things, but I just can't. Teachers always expect me to be one of the top kids in the class. Every year. Mom and Dad always expect me to get really good grades, too. It is a lot of pressure.

I love the way I can fall asleep during the summer without having to worry about school.

It's because you're smart, but they will love you even if you do get a bad grade. Max! Trust me. I know!!

Now I am already getting stressed. Not good. I can't sleep when I'm stressed!

Plus, 5th graders have to deal with the worst possible teacher in the whole school: Mrs. Buda.

She is pure evil.

HA!
That
looks
just
like
her!

Everyone at school knows she's the worst. There are so many teachers at school, and they all smile at you in the halls, say nice things to you, and seem like they actually like kids. On the other hand, she gives a ton of homework, her tests are impossible, and I am 98% sure that she doesn't even like kids. I really, really hope that we don't get her this year.

Maggie is not even worried. I don't
think she understands that our whole
school year could be torture if we get
a really bad teacher. I don't think I am
going to be able to sleep at night, I am
so worried about it. I wish I could be
like Maggie and not care, but it's
impossible.

Yes I am!

I just
know I
can't
pick my
teacher,
so I
have to
deal with
whomever
we get. Why get
stressed about
something you
can't change.
Max?

Now about this back-to-school
shopping. Clothes shopping is the worst.
It is torture, especially with my mom and my
sister. They take forever. I mean, how hard
is it to pick a new shirt or a pair of pants?
Plus, Maggie is always complaining that her
clothes are uncomfortable. I really do not
understand. To me, clothes are clothes.
I could wear any old pair
of jeans. Not Maggie. She
would try on thousands of
pairs of jeans until she
finds the absolutely
perfect pair that fits like
they were made
just for her.

The best part of back-to-school shopping is the stuff. The stuff: school supplies! We always get all-new stuff for school — backpacks, paper, pens, folders, and all that stuff. There's nothing like starting the school year out right with a brand-new notebook, brand-new pens, and a totally organized mind. That's the best.

When we shop with Mom, she picks out pens that are basic, normal pens. She looks at the price of everything. She buys plain yellow pencils. BORING. Plain pink rectangle erasers. BORING. Not that I don't appreciate her getting us all that stuff, but it's just plain BORING. I didn't even know they sold that regular stuff anymore.

Now if Dad is shopping for school supplies with us, it's a whole different kind of adventure.
Back-to-school shopping with Dad is the best!! (Sorry Mom!)

Hello. I am a boring yellow pencil. Your mom loves me.

Dad finds the coolest, weirdest pens and he lets us get them, like pens that have different color ink, pens with secret voice recorders on them, pens that have a secret note compartment that you can use to hold secret messages. Cool stuff. We get cool pencil cases, and the most awesome markers and folders. We're pretty much stylin' when it comes to school supplies. Plus, Dad always lets us get extra cool stuff that is not on the list.

That was the COOLEST

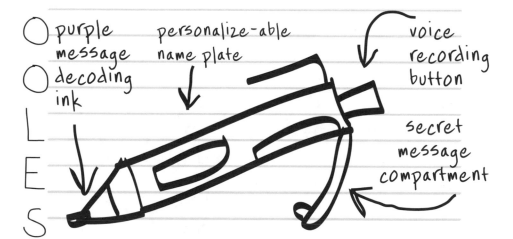

purple message decoding ink

personalize-able name plate

voice recording button

secret message compartment

OK, so I am looking forward to getting new school supplies...

...but I am not looking forward to going back to school! Noooooooooooo! I don't want to go back to school!

HELP! SAVE ME!

My brain seriously hurts just thinking about it. Ugh.

Things You Need for School:

1. Clothes - in the new styles, of course!

2. Brand-new, fresh writing paper and brand-new notebooks.

3. Fun pencils and gel pens!
   Yes! FUN stuff!

4. The big box of 128 crayons.
   Please, please, please!

5. New shoes!

6. Glue - for making glue puddles on your desk (it's so cool when they dry!).

7. Heavy paper for making killer airplanes.

8. Paper clips, because you can never have too many.
   You and your silly paper clips!

9. New, clean, not-ripped backpack. (You know, the kind that doesn't smell like moldy string cheese and rotten bologna.)
   GROSS!

It's almost over!
It's almost over!

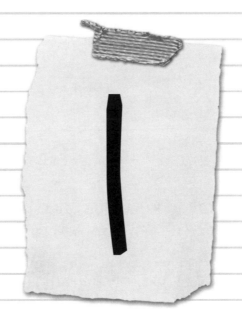

Woo hoo!
The end of the journal is right
around the corner!!!

Hooray!

What I Learned from Writing This Summer
By Max (The World's Coolest Brother)

Guess what? Mom picked our last topic. I don't think Maggie or I would ever write about what we learned from writing, but OK.

Journal time is almost officially over. At least it will be after I write today. I am so sad about it. (Ha ha). Today I am supposed to spend some time thinking about what makes me a good brother, and why I am lucky to have a twin sister. I know I'm a good brother for a million reasons, but I guess I have to write about the top five. Fine. It will be tough, but I will try to narrow it down. I mean, just look how awesome I am to begin with...hee hee...

OK, seriously, drumroll please...

TOP 5 Reasons Why Maggie Is Lucky to Have Me –

Thank you.

1. I do not play practical jokes on Maggie. I have whoopee cushions, itching powder, snapping gum, and about a million other practical joke gags, and I'm not afraid to use them, just not on Maggie.

And if you EVER do, I will show EVERYONE that picture of you in that pink tutu.

2. I have never shown anyone that picture of Maggie in the bathtub that Mom took when she was 5 because she was "so adorable."

The key word here is "try."

3. I (try) not to make fun of the girly things she does, like painting her nails, curling her hair, dressing up in girl clothes, and shopping.

4. Even though Maggie thinks I snoop around her room when she is not around, I really don't. Good. You better not! DO

most times (hee hee)

5. I am never boring. I may annoy her, and bug her, and drive her a little crazy ~~sometimes~~ but she'll never be bored with me around!

very true.

Maggie is lucky to have me as a brother.

Now, why I am lucky to have a twin That's nice! sister... that is definitely harder. Hmmmm...NOT!

I guess the first reason is that it is good to have someone to hang out with all the time. It would be boring to spend every day alone.

Plus, it's nice to be the same age. I don't know what I would do if my sister was True. a tiny baby who couldn't talk or if she was a True. high-schooler who ignored me. That would NO probably stink. babies.please!

And Maggie, you better not get too crazy when you read this, but Maggie is pretty cool. Sure, she's annoying sometimes (aren't we all), but she is also fun to be around a lot of the time. She makes me laugh. Clearly, I've trained her well to be a cool sister. I guess we should keep her.

Thanks a lot. Max!

The End! The End!

The End of my journal!!!!!

The End

• Summer

What I Learned from Writing This Summer   By Maggie

Today is my last journal day. Mom just said so this morning. Woo hoo! Mom said I should make a list of at least 5 reasons that Max should be glad to have me as a sister. and why I am glad to have a twin brother. He should be VERY glad he has me. so that part should be easy. (:

5 reasons why MAX is lucky to have me:

1 I do not make fun of Max at school. even when he gets all stressed out (which is actually pretty funny. but still. I never make fun of him).   **Yeah, that is not funny.**

2 Everyone knows that it's totally icky to "like" your friend's brother. I keep Max safe from all my friends who might otherwise be "boy crazy" for him. Trust me. they tend to get really crazy when it comes to boys.

I'm sure they are crazy for me anyway, but thanks.

(continued on the next page)

3 I go to watch all of Max's baseball and basketball games and don't complain (at least not that much).

4 I don't like leftover food, so Max always gets the leftovers. I will always save those things for Max. And Max LOVES leftovers.

Yep. Sure do!

5 I stand up for Max when other kids act like jerks (for example, the Bulldogs). It's OK for me to mess with my brother, but I'm not going to put up with other people messing with him.

I could go on, but as you can see, Max is very lucky to have me.

Wait a minute, it's OK for you to mess with me? I don't think so!

I would love for you to go on. I'd like to read more!

Why I am lucky to have Max as a twin brother? Now that is a little more difficult. **HEY!**

Ha! Just kidding. **Awwwww!** Max really is a great brother. He is funny, so that is good. It makes things more interesting when he's around.

I will say that I don't think I learned anything new about Max by writing this journal, but I did enjoy the funny pictures and things that he drew along the way!!

I really didn't mind writing this over the summer. Sometimes I didn't feel like writing, but when I read it later, I was glad I did. Plus, it gave me another place to draw!! I may actually miss writing this now that it's over.

HEY! Don't be giving Mom any ideas here!

THE END

Best Part of the Summer:
by Maggie

The best part of summer was getting ice cream EVERY DAY!!!! I had sundaes, cones, milkshakes, those little frozen-ball ice cream things, ice cream sandwiches, ice cream bars, and every other kind of ice cream you can think of!!! One day, the ice cream truck came down my street and I had to run out of the house and chase after it for 5 houses until I finally caught it. Thank goodness!

Wait - what is this? I thought we were done writing!?!?!

UGH!

You must love writing, Maggie!

Mmm. Breakfast in bed. Perfect.

Yeah, right! Mom would never go for that!

I'm so glad that Dad shares my love for ice cream. I can always count on him to splurge with me!

Ick. I don't know how you guys eat so much ice cream!

This is what could happen because of Maggie's love of ice cream:

Max's Best Summer Moment

    My last baseball game of the season.
Last inning. Bases loaded. Two outs.
We're down by 3 runs. And I am up.
To be honest – I was terrified that I
would strike out and let down my team.

Me = Super nervous

Braden = Annoying

Me = Bored

But I connected with the first pitch,
and hit way into the outfield.

Me hitting it

I ran as fast as I could. I got a triple!

Me cheering for you!
(I really did!)

Run Max!
Go Max!
Yay Max!

Me running my butt off

My teammates jumped all over me and cheered and it was AWESOME!!!!!

Me being told by my team how awesome I am.

...and that was really the end of this thing called the summer journal.

THE END

BYE!

Maggie, who are you saying "bye" to?

Oh, just be quiet, Max.

Use the
following pages
to start your
own journal.

Have fun!

You can print more
journal pages at:
www.MomMadeUsWriteThis.com

Actually it
← is fun.

Make a list of things you would
write about in your journal...brainstorm!

1.

2.

3.

4.

5.

6.

7.

8.

9.

10.

Summer

Would you like to share a journal
with someone, like I did with Maggie?
If so, who?

Would your mom make you write a journal?

What would
your journal
cover look
like? Draw it
here. →

What is your favorite thing to do
with your family?

Draw a picture of your family members.

What is the funniest thing that happened to you this summer?

Summer

Summer

Summer

Summer

ACKNOWLEDGEMENTS

I would like to send my heartfelt thank you to those people who were invaluable to me during the production of this book. Mark, M&M, Joanna, Melanie, Jeff, Brian, Monica and Tami — I feel very blessed to have all of you in my life.

ABOUT THE AUTHOR

Ali Maier was born in Johnstown, PA, and grew up in Upper St. Clair, just south of Pittsburgh. Ali now lives in a Cleveland (OH) suburb with her husband, two children and her mini lop bunny 'Angel'. Ali has a BA in Elementary Education from John Carroll University. She loves spending time with her family, reading, writing, kayaking and paddle boarding on Lake Erie. Ali loves to travel with her family, and has visited 16 different countries and many places in the beautiful USA.

ABOUT THE ILLUSTRATOR

Joanna Robinson Ph.D. is a writer, editor, education professional, illustrator, and designer with a passion for creating silly, engaging, and challenging children's educational content. Joanna has written and illustrated exciting children's content for Sesame Workshop, Nick Jr., LeapFrog, Encyclopedia Britannica, Farfaria, Red Apple Reading, and many others. Joanna lives with her husband and three cats just outside of Cleveland Ohio.